Super '70s

Cars of the Disco Decade

Patrick R. Foster

Published by

kp
since
1952

**krause
publications**

700 East State St., Iola, WI 54990-0001
715-445-2214
www.krause.com

Please, call or write us for our free catalog of antiques and collectibles publications.
To place an order or receive our free catalog, call 800-258-0929. For editorial comment and further information,
use our regular business telephone at (715) 445-2214

Library of Congress Catalog Number: 00-101577
ISBN: 0-87341-902-2

Printed in the United States of America

Contents

Dedication

This book is dedicated to the memory of my brother Michael.
He was a wonderful human being and he truly loved life. His smiling eyes and mischievous grin were the trademarks of a man who delighted in friendships. His vitality and good spirit, his thoughtfulness and his generosity will long be remembered.
No man was ever prouder of his family than he.
And we all miss him terribly.

Foreword

Ah, the Seventies! The decade seemed perfectly ripe with promise. In the previous ten years Americans had witnessed more changes in the social convention and order than had been seen in the prior 50 years. Women's rights had come to the forefront, integration and the civil rights movement had finally corrected many past injustices, and prosperity reigned throughout the land. The 1960s had been a time to enjoy life, and the decade to follow seemed bound to be even better.

Yet, like so many other plans we made, things didn't turn out quite the way we thought they would. Society changed, yes, but not always for the better. Cars got better, then worse, then better again. Vast economic forces which were never dreamed of in earlier decades came to the forefront in the mid-1970s to produce a cataclysmic change in our way of life. Thousands of businesses were closed, millions of people were thrown out of work and the wealth of nations disappeared. It seemed like the country was on the verge of an immense depression, one that many people feared might last forever.

It was a turbulent time.

Yet, like most things that happen in America, in the end the good outweighed the bad and today we look back on this decade with fondness. As a time in our nation's history, it presented many challenges. As a time in our own lives, it was memorable indeed.

Few history books spring forth from the mind or hands of a single person and there are many people who deserve mention for helping make *Super '70s* possible. First of all, my thanks to kind and generous Ron Kowalke of Krause Publications, a friend who has spared no pains in supporting my efforts. I'd especially like to mention Jay Cowperthwaite and Leo Carroll, two friends who are fellow survivors of the 1970s. Bill Wilson gave me valuable advice, as did Bob Smith, Jimmy Dunn and a host of other friends. Most of the photos used in this book came from the extensive files of Krause Publications and The Patrick R. Foster Historical Collection. However, a few other sources provided us with needed pictures, including Elliot Kahn, Ron Kowalke and Diane Montville. As usual, two of my favorite literature suppliers, John Wimble and John Ziemer, rose to the occasion with top quality photos, catalogs and background materials.

My editor and associate, Jo Phillip, did an outstanding job keeping everything on track and on time and I'd like to give her recognition and thanks for the hard work, good advice and strong advocacy she displayed.

I'd especially like to thank my extended family, many of whom have put up with me for over 40 years. This includes my siblings and their spouses; my brother, Will, and his wife, Maureen; David and his wife, Tracey; Dan and his wife, Jeannine; my sister-in-law, Cheryl Foster; my sister, Sylvia, and her husband, John Longo; and my big sister Diane, who more than anyone nurtured in me a love of reading. That passion for reading led me, naturally enough, to a career in writing, which has been a great joy.

I've been married twenty years now and I'm very happy to say my wife and I share a love that grows sweeter every year. Our beautiful daughter, Caitlin, has grown to be quite an accomplished artist and I confidently predict her fame will someday outshine my own by a large measure. God put these wonderful people in my life and I will be forever grateful.

Finally, I want to thank my ever-loyal readers, who have faithfully followed me from one book to the next, always willing to consider a new idea or a new approach. Without you marvelous readers I would be stuck somewhere, bored beyond telling, doing some job I really didn't want to do. Thank you for saving me from that.

Patrick Foster
October 2000

About the Author

What a career this man has had! Patrick Foster as enjoyed the past ten years or so doing what he loves best — writing about cars, trucks and Jeep vehicles. His work has earned him many awards, making him one of America's best-known automotive writers. Pat's many previous books-*American Motors-The Last Independent*, *The Story of Jeep*, *The Nash Styling Sketchbook*, and *The Metropolitan Story* have all won critical acclaim, as did *Mister Javelin — Guy Hadsall Jr. at American Motors*, on which Pat worked as editor. In 1996 The Society of Automotive Historians awarded him the prestigious **Carl Benz Award** for the Best Periodical Article written during the previous year. In 1999 the Antique Automobile Club of America bestowed the **Thomas McKean Memorial Cup** — its famous award for best book- for *The Story of Jeep*.

Pat Foster, circa 1971 — at the beginning of the Super Seventies.

Patrick Foster — the 2000 model. "I'm not as young as I used to be (Who Is?) but my love of cars has grown stronger over the years".

Chapter One

1970

GM Strikes Out

Is there anything more exciting than the first year of a new decade? The dawn of an era always seems to hold so much promise, so many chances for real improvement in the human condition. The 1960s had seen a social and cultural revolution, with the status of women and minorities substantially changing. In the new decade of the 1970s, it seemed likely their conditions would improve even more. After all, the great social conscience of the people had been mightily elevated and was hardly likely to retreat. Things were bound to get even better in the new age unfolding.

Not that all was pastoral bliss in 1970. Hard fighting was still going on in Vietnam. The streets of our nation's capital were often filled with citizens demonstrating against that unpopular conflict. One result was the great human tragedy that occurred out at a state university in Ohio, when four student protesters were shot dead by jittery

National Guard troops who were no older than the kids they fired on.

Richard Milhous Nixon was in the White House, and he was still an extremely popular president. The scandalous events that would later force him from office and tarnish his name forever had not yet occurred.

Inventors and engineers were thriving that year. The first liquid crystal display was patented and the first pocket calculator was devised. Boeing's fantastic 747, the first of the so-called Jumbo Jets, went into service on the New York-to-Europe run. And writers were also thriving in 1970—dissident Russian novelist Aleksandr Solzhenitsyn was awarded the Nobel Prize for Literature.

George C. Scott gave an outstanding performance in the title role of the movie *Patton*, a monumental film that won Academy Awards for Best Actor as well as Best Picture that year, nudging out the

Chevrolet restyled its popular Chevelle for 1970, including the legendary SS 396, one of the best-loved muscle cars of all time.

A dynamic model in Chevy's mid-size line was this Malibu Sport four-door pillarless hardtop, a beautiful body style we wish they still made today.

In the Fall of 1969, Chevy's all-new 1970 Camaro wasn't quite ready, so '69-style Camaros like this were offered as early 1970 models in the interim.

The early '70 Camaros were soon superseded by the all-new mid-1970 Camaro shown here—a style that would remain in production throughout the decade. Note the model's trendy hairdo and minidress.

Three views of Chevy's exciting new Camaro reveal its clean lines and sports appeal.

A bold new product for Chevrolet this year was the stunning beautiful Monte Carlo.

immensely popular three-hankie movie *Love Story,* which starred Ryan O'Neil and Ali MacGraw.

Detroit was coming off a very good prior year (1969), but sales during the first year of the new decade were running at a much slower clip—mainly because of a 65-day strike at General Motors. It was too bad—the General fielded an impressive lineup of new cars for 1970. Chevrolet introduced a completely restyled Chevelle at the regular fall announcement and followed it up in February 1970 with an all-new and dramatically beautiful Camaro. An even more important debut was a new nameplate that marked Chevy's entrance into the "personal luxury market"—the fabulous Monte Carlo. The Monte Carlo was about the size of a typical U.S. intermediate of that era, but was lavishly trimmed and elegantly appointed. Available only as a two-door hardtop, it quickly captured the public's heart. Monte Carlo became one of the signature cars of the 1970s—a symbol of the decade itself—and Chevrolet has been trying to recapture its allure ever since.

At the low end of Chevy's model range was a very popular family compact, the Nova. Most people have forgotten that in 1970. Chevy's Nova was still available with a four-cylinder engine. However, since it was priced only about $78 less than the six-cylinder version, the four didn't appeal to most buyers and only 2,247 were built for the U.S. market, versus over 170,000 Nova sixes, and 139,000 Nova V-8s. Of the latter, a 307-cid V-8 was usually fitted, though Nova SS models offered a 350-cube engine, and even the 396-cid mill could be had on special order.

Ford had a line of slightly restyled full-size cars to show, but the big news had come the previous year with the debut of its new Maverick small car. Although the faithful old Falcon compact returned for 1970, it was greatly overshadowed by its lower-priced and heavily advertised Maverick stablemate. Maverick offered a single body style, a two-door sedan on a 103-inch wheelbase, priced as before at $1,995. The combination of low price, decent style, solid—if uninspired—engineering and mass advertising made the Maverick one of the biggest hits of the year, with 451,081 1970 models built. By mid-year the old-style Falcon was gone, replaced by a new Falcon based on the longer 117-inch wheelbase Fairlane chassis, becoming a budget-priced intermediate in the process. The entire Fairlane line came in for a complete re-styling and looked much

1970

Top News Items

- American involvement in Southeast Asia expands when Richard Nixon sends troops into Cambodia.

- 10,000 women celebrate 50 years of voting rights with a parade in New York City.

- National Guardsmen kill four students at Kent State University after firing into a crowd of protesters.

Three views of Chevrolet Nova for 1970. Although this particular car has a 307 V8 (note engine emblem on front fender) in 1970 Nova even offered a four cylinder engine!

In 1970, the most popular automobiles were big (or so-called full-sized) cars. And for those big car lovers, Buick offered a wide range of vehicles including this sporty Buick Wildcat hardtop.

lower and sleeker than before. The intermediate-sized Torino, formerly a trim series, became a separate model this year, though still based on the Fairlane. Ford's stylish Thunderbird series came in three models, a regular two-door hardtop, a Landau hardtop, and a Landau four-door model.

Another hit car from Ford that was returning for its second model year was the extraordinarily beautiful Lincoln Continental Mark III. Its sharply chiseled lines and bold, upright chrome grille had set the luxury coupe market on its ear during its debut season, so the physical changes for 1970 were few. More alterations could be noticed on the regular Continentals, the big four-door sedan and the two-door hardtop, both of which were restyled this year. The new look was more massive, heavier and somewhat baroque.

Most of Chrysler's full-size 300 series cars were equipped with a potent 350-horsepower 440-cid V-8 mill, but the extra-special 300H (Hurst) came with a massaged engine that was good for 375 horsepower. This amount of power was needed, because the Chrysler, like all American luxury cars back then, was enormous. Its dimensions are almost breathtaking to recall—124-inch wheelbase, and 224.7 inches

1970
Top Movies

- Love Story
- Airport
- M*A*S*H*
- Patton
- The Aristocats

bumper to bumper. It was what kids referred to as a "boat," but it flew down the road.

Although it wasn't announced at the time, 1970 would be the last year a buyer could order a full-size Chrysler convertible. The 2,201 customers fortunate enough to get one were lucky indeed. The Imperial, a lineup entirely separate from the standard Chrysler line, was the corporation's most prestigious product that year. The Imperial featured

Monte Carlo was easily the richest-looking Chevy that year, and helped popularize the category of cars known as mid-size luxury coupes.

Also stunning was the great actor George C. Scott, shown here as he appeared in the movie "Patton". Scott won the Oscar for Best Actor for his performance.

One of America's favorite cop shows was "Adam-12". In retrospect it seems strange that in the age of Muscle Cars, a TV show about police would be so popular.

Chevy's Impala still offered a beautiful convertible model.

The popular Caprice series included this good-looking two door hardtop.

American Motors Corporation bought Kaiser Jeep, renamed it Jeep Corporation, and set about to improve Jeep's performance, quality and sales.

At new car announcement time, American Motors introduced the new Hornet two- and four-door sedans, which replaced the discontinued Rambler line.

the lavishly appointed Crown series, which included both four-door hardtops (1,333 built) and two-door hardtops (254 built).

The popular Dodge Dart featured aggressive new styling. The line included a handsome four-door sedan, as well as a body style that, though once one of the best-selling, isn't offered nowadays—the two-door hardtop. Although the Dart sedan was a neatly packaged family car, the visual appeal of the Dart Swinger hardtop made that model the most popular

1970

Top TV Shows

• Marcus Welby, M.D.

• The Flip Wilson Show

• Here's Lucy

• Ironside

• Gunsmoke

• The ABC Movie of the Week

• Hawaii Five-O

• Medical Center

• Bonanza

• The F.B.I.

Dart by a huge margin. The line also included the hot Dart Swinger 340, a potent hardtop powered by a 275-horsepower 340-cid V-8.

Dodge's Coronet had new front-end sheet metal for 1970, replacing the old full-width grille with a bold new front that featured two oval-shaped openings. Each opening was framed by chrome bumpers, for a remarkably attractive effect. Rear sheet metal was also restyled. The legendary Hemi R/T returned, though only 14 were built. This was, as it happened, the final year for the Coronet R/T, and also the last year a Coronet convertible would be offered.

Dodge finally got its own ponycar that year, the stunning Challenger. Offered in two body styles, hardtop and convertible, and in three series, base, R/T and T/A, the Challenger was a long-overdue response to the Mustang, Javelin and Camaro.

Plymouth's popular Valiant sedan was carried over with minor changes, but was joined this year by the new Duster coupe. The idea behind the Duster was that it would offer a sportier, more youthful appearance than a regular two-door sedan, and it did. With prices beginning at less than $2,200, it couldn't help but sell. The Plymouth Division had some other exciting new offerings, like the aggressively styled Plymouth Barracuda pony-car. However, the hottest model in the red-hot Plymouth line-up was the fantastic Superbird, with its sky-high tail wing. Built on the Roadrunner chassis, the Superbird's 440-cid mill offered either a screaming 375-horsepower with 4 bbl carb, or 390-horsepower with a three 2 bbl set-up. And a total of 135 were equipped with a rampaging dual-quad

America's Sports Car—the red-hot Corvette—was available in coupe and convertible models this year.

426-cid Hemi, blasting out an astonishing 425 horsepower! Subtle it was not.

For 1970, American Motors had a lot of product news—a very modern-looking Hornet compact, which replaced the Rambler; and also the first American subcompact car, the Gremlin, which it introduced on April Fool's Day. The Hornet was available in both two- and four-door sedans, with either six or V-8 engines, while the diminutive Gremlin came only as a six-cylinder two-door. The lowest priced Gremlin was, at $1,879, the least expensive American car on the market—at least from a major manufacturer. The Gremlin stands today as one of the major landmarks in the history of the American automotive industry—the first U.S. subcompact.

The AMX, America's only other two-seat sports car, was given a new grille and new hood, looking more modern now but losing some of the purity of line that the original enjoyed. This would be the last year for a separate AMX series, and the last year that it would be a two-seater. AMC's Javelin pony-car also returned, and this year offered, in addition to the base and SST series, a limited edition Trans Am replica, as well as a Mark Donahue edition. Performance evidently was a hot idea at AMC for 1970, because the smallest of the American companies also introduced a muscle car version of its stalwart

Rebel intermediate. The Rebel Machine was a joint effort of AMC and the redoubtable Hurst Performance. Its specifications included a 390-cid, 340-horsepower V-8, four-speed transmission, hood mounted tach, Hurst shifter, power disc brakes, and more. Offered in eye-catching paint schemes, it was one of the most noticeable cars on the road, and went a long way toward changing AMC's image in the minds of gearheads.

Also making industry headlines was AMC's gutsy purchase of Kaiser Jeep Corporation. Jeep was an also-ran in the U.S. market, selling fewer than 50,000 units per year, living off its past glories, and making money only on its military and overseas business. AMC Chairman, Roy D. Chapin, Jr. was certain his company could turn

Hornet's front-end appearance was trim and very modern-looking.

Not content to live on economy-car sales alone, AMC continued to offer its high performance AMX two-seater.

Jeep into a sales success in the U.S. retail market. It was a tall order.

Buick was showing off a restyled Skylark—crisper and sportier than the previous years' offerings. The big Buick Le Sabre, one of America's premier family cars, featured only mildly updated styling, as did the division's other full-size offerings, the Electra 225—which high-schoolers

On April 1, 1970, AMC introduced its newest idea—the Gremlin, which was America's first subcompact car. Priced as low as $1879 for the two-seat model, Gremlin was an instant hit with buyers.

dubbed the "deuce and a quarter," and the Wildcat, which was in its final year. Buick's Riviera was also only modestly changed, mainly because an all-new Riv was being prepared for the following year.

Auto emission regulations were still in their infancy in 1970, relegated mainly to the use of simple PCV (positive crankcase ventilation) valves fitted onto existing valve covers, which routed crankcase fumes into the carburetor, where they could be burned in the cylinders. It didn't cut emissions all that much, but it didn't cut horsepower either, so the Muscle Cars of 1970 really had muscle. And they were still very popular, though their days were numbered. Every company and just about every division had them—Mercury had its Cyclone GT, Pontiac had its veteran GTO, Chevy went into battle with its Chevelle Super Sport, Ford fielded the mighty Torino GT and GT Cobra, and of course the legendary Boss Mustang. Little AMC had its hot Rebel Machine, and even Jeep had a couple of "hot" cars—the V-6 powered Hurst Jeepster Special and the limited production Renegade I. Oldsmobile, of course, had its 442 series.

Imported cars, which nearly everybody still referred to as "foreign cars," had a good year in 1970. Volkswagen was the undisputed king of imports, with its Beetle selling over 500,000 units in the US. Toyota was a distant second at 184,898 cars sold—Americans were still leery of anything built in Japan. Indeed, the phrase "made in Japan" was considered a put-down, with extremely negative connotations as to the quality of workmanship and materials.

Some other imports that were popular then are just memories today—wonderful old cars like the MG and Triumph sports cars, the quirky Fiat sedans and sports cars, the weird French Renaults, Simcas and Citroens, and the solid, though underrated, Opel line from Germany. Here in the U.S., Opels were retailed by Buick dealers, and company advertising referred to them as "Buick-Opel dealers."

Not that America didn't have a few odd cars of its own. Out in Kalamazoo Michigan, Checker Motors was still turning out its taxi cabs and Marathon passenger cars, all with styling that came right out of the 1950s. Meanwhile, in Athens, Ohio, King Midget—even though suffering financial difficulties—managed to bring out a new model to supplement its existing little one-cylinder roadster. The previous year's model, a steel-bodied two-seater, is referred to now as the third series King Midget. It was joined by an all-new King Midget, fitted with a one-piece fiberglass body that looked very much like a dune buggy. The King Midgets were tiny and strange, but they got almost 90 miles to a gallon of gas and they were the cheapest "car" you could

1970
Music News

- The Beatles break up—their last film "Let it Be" premiers May 20.
- "American Top 40" debuts with Casey Kasem as host.
- Soundtrack albums sell well this year. The "Woodstock" "Easy Rider" and "Butch Cassidy and the Sundance Kid" records fly off the shelves.

buy—though they were usually available only via mail-order. Sadly, a fire broke out in the King Midget plant, destroying the dies for the new fiberglass model after only a handful were built. Faced with financial losses and slow sales of the older, steel-bodied King Midget, the company soon folded.

But there was good news in South Bend, Indiana. The Avanti Motors company was still hand-assembling the high-powered Avanti II for the more cultivated buyer, and was enjoying good sales. Available only in a single two-door model, the Avanti could be ordered in virtually any color on earth and just about any interior trim, too. The factory was happy to oblige special requests—for a fee, of course.

Things were changing in 1970. That year's Miss America contest saw the first black woman to compete in the national pageant—Cheryl Brown, Miss Iowa. The crown, however, went to Pam Eldred of Bloomfield, Michigan. Ford's new Torino won *Motor Trend's* "Car of the Year" award.

There were tragic stories as well. Janis Joplin and Jimi Hendrix, two of America's most popular rock stars, died within weeks of one another—both of drug overdoses.

America was still enjoying "Gunsmoke", one of the longest running shows on TV. We also watched "The Flip Wilson Show", a popular comedy, and the cop shows "Adam-12" and "Hawaii Five-0". "Marcus Welby, M.D." seemed to have the entire country glued to the tube.

So, 1970 was a good year for products—but an off year for sales. Sales of cars and light trucks fell more than a million from 1969—down to 9,850,276. The drop was almost entirely GM's loss, the result of a strike by its workers. Sales of imports increased by more than 200,000 units.

It certainly wasn't the best way to start a new decade.

One of the strongest Muscle cars on the market was this Rebel "Machine" from AMC.

A very unique car of the 1970s was this Chrysler 300H, a muscle car built on a full-size luxury car chassis. Modifications were handled by Hurst Performance Corporation. The 300H featured a fiber glass power bulge hood with air scoop, plus a fiber glass rear deck with spoiler.

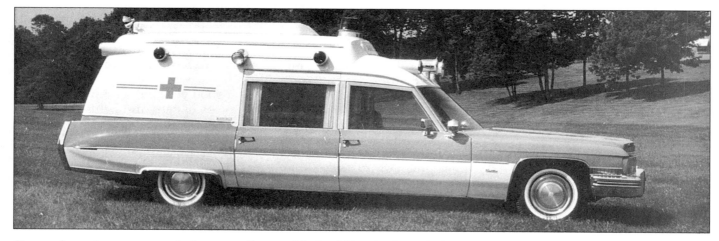

Remember when every ambulance on the road looked like this? Back then, Cadillac offered a commercial car chassis that was extremely popular with companies that built ambulances, limousines and funeral cars.

Cadillac was considered the Standard of the World back then, and Caddy's Coupe DeVille was the most coveted luxury car in the world.

Buick offered this dandy Skylark Custom four-door hardtop. In 1970, Skylark was still part of Buick's mid-size line. In later years, it would drop down to a compact chassis.

Buick offered a muscle car in 1970, this gorgeous GS 455, powered by a killer 455-cid V8. This was sort of a hot rod for the mature (or rather, semi-mature) driver. The GS 455 was also available in a convertible model.

Dodge was pushing its performance image this year and offered a broad range of hot cars. The Swinger hardtop was a sporty version of the compact Dart line.

Dodge finally offered its own ponycar this year, the handsome Challenger. It was available as a two-door hardtop coupe or convertible. Three series were offered: base, R/T and T/A.

Dodge Coronet featured bold new front styling this year. Shown here is racing great Mark Donahue in a Coronet 500 convertible.

Hottest of the Coronet line was this Super Bee. Note the mean-looking twin hood scoops, bold new grille and special striping on the quarter panel.

Two versions of the Dodge Charger, the regular Charger (bottom) and the hotter-performing Charger R/T (top).

Three views of Ford's hot-selling Maverick. The two light-colored cars are standard Mavericks, while the darker car is a Grabber sport model.

Ford's Torino became a separate model this year—and was named Motor Trend's Car Of The Year. Shown is the Torino GT.

At the beginning of the year, Ford's Falcon looked much as it had the year before, but by mid-year the Falcon was switched over to the mid-size Torino chassis (See inset).

Other Ford models this year included the new Torino four-door hardtop (top), and the Ford Thunderbird (bottom).

Besides the regular two-door coupe, Ford's Mustang could also be had as a fastback coupe, or as a sharp convertible.

Ford's standard-size offerings included this basic Galaxie 500 four-door sedan (top) and the pretty LTD Brougham two-door hardtop (bottom).

Returning this year was Lincoln's stunningly beautiful Mark III, a luxury two-door coupe that was the class of the market.

Mercury's regular lineup included a muscle car, too—the dramatic-looking Cyclone GT.

Always willing to muscle in on the Muscle Car market was Oldsmobile, which fielded the terrific 4-4-2, available this year as a two door Holiday (hardtop) Coupe, a Sports Coupe (pillar) and a Convertible. A W30 package continued as a special performance package on the 4-4-2 and included a 455-cid 4 barrel V-8 with high-lift cam. The W-30 also included the fiberglass hood with air scoops shown here.

The Delta Eighty-Eight Holiday four-door hardtop was one of the more attractive models in Olds' family car line.

Plymouth's Valiant line was joined this year by the new Duster coupe, which came in several variations. Shown here is the regular Duster two-door, (bottom and middle), joined by the hot Duster 340 V8 (top), raciest of the Duster line.

Plymouth's Barracuda was a sharp-looking entry in the ponycar field.

The Roadrunner was hard to ignore. If the loud colors, hot performing and eye-grabbing stripes didn't get your attention, the Roadrunner's "beep-beep" horn did.

The hottest of the Plymouth line this year was the thunderous Plymouth Super Bird, a custom-built hot rod that was one of the greatest road-burners of the decade.

Pontiac's new Firebird Formula 400 included a 400-cube V8 with dual exhausts.

For many a driver, the rear view was the most common one they got of the new Firebird.

The Avanti was still in production, built not by Studebaker but by a small company called Avanti Motors Corporation.

Pontiac's "goat," the GTO, was still running strong and featured a front end cap made of a dent-resistant Endura material.

Pontiac's big cars shared a common styling theme this year, a huge classic-style grille that seemed to recall the classic Duesenburg.

The King Midget automobile had debuted in the years just after WWII and the firm, Midget Motors of Athens, Ohio, continued to build cars though the 1950s and '60s. The final year for King Midget cars was 1970. That year, a new style appeared (top). Referred to by historians as the fourth series, this model utilized a fiberglass body that resembled the dune buggy kit cars that were then popular. The very last King Midget car built, however, is reported to have been this third series steel-bodied car.

Chapter Two

1971

Culture Clash—Muscle Cars Meet The New Subcompacts

Everyone knew the American subcompacts were coming—heck, most of us wanted them to arrive quickly, if for no other reason than to stem the flow of imported cars. The mystery that surrounded their development, the rumors that flew back and forth about how they would look, how they would drive and how much they would cost, all lent an air of tremendous excitement.

And in our hearts, many of us knew that the days of the Muscle Cars were nearly over. High insurance costs were a big factor in their reduced popularity, but if truth is told, the whole performance thing had gotten out of hand. Selling 400 horsepower rocket sleds to teenagers no longer seemed to make much sense. And, there were other compelling reasons. Times were changing, and

kids' interest in fuel economy and clean air was supplanting their interest in carburetors and camshafts. The contrast between two philosophies, power versus economy, was never more clearly drawn than in 1971. Although Muscle Cars were still hot news, the Ford Pinto and Chevy Vega had arrived on the scene.

With its strike settled and automobile production in full swing, GM came roaring back into the marketplace. The biggest news that year, naturally, was the Chevy Vega, the first American subcompact car from GM, and a symbol of the General's leadership in design, styling and production technologies. The Vega, you must understand, was GM's strongest effort to date to build and sell small cars profitably in the U.S. All new, the Vega was offered in four two-

Few people recall that Steven Spielberg's first major movie was 1971's "Duel," a landmark film that was also a pretty thrilling movie.

Jeep introduced the Renegade II, which featured gorgeous alloy wheels, stripes, and a potent V6 engine.

One of the rarest and most collectable Jeep vehicles of all is the Hurst Jeepster, produced only in 1971, in small numbers.

AMC unveiled a new hot-rod this year, the thundering Hornet SC360. Powered by a 245-horsepower 360-cid V8, this specialty car was priced at a low $2663.

Remember this guy? The masked state trooper endorsed the safety and gas mileage benefits of BF Goodrich's Lifesaver Radial tires. According to the ad, the trooper had to wear a mask because "neither the trooper nor his state can lend their names to any product."

door models, a notchback sedan (starting at $2090), a hatchback coupe ($2196), station wagon ($2328), and a commercial/delivery version of the wagon ($2138), all on a 97-inch wheelbase. Vegas were powered by a radical, all-new overhead cam four-cylinder engine with two design features that set it apart from the crowd—an aluminum alloy block without the usual iron cylinder liners and, oddly enough, a cast-iron head, employed for cost reasons. It was an unusual move to include an iron head on an alloy block, and the different rates of expansion between the two would prove troublesome. Later, the alloy block and the head gasket would be numbered as the most common source of mechanical troubles in what would prove to be one of the most problem-plagued automobiles ever built in America. The Vega, you see, was a veritable disaster, but that fact wouldn't become clear for a few more years.

Ford took a different tack, designing its new Pinto subcompact along more conservative lines. Pinto engines were basic cast iron block/cast iron head designs, with good power, good fuel economy and decent reliability, but generally lacking the exotic materials and design that made auto writers sit up and take notice. Pinto offered two models—a basic two-door sedan starting at $1919 and a hatchback sedan, stickered at $2,062.

1971

Top News Items

- George McGovern, a South Dakota Senator, announces he will run as a Democratic candidate in the 1972 presidential election.

- Idi Amin seizes power in Uganda.

- A survey shows that over one-third of U.S. college students have tried marijuana.

- Voting gets younger: the voting age is lowered from 21 to 18.

- Soft contact lenses make their debut in the marketplace.

- China launches its first space satellite.

The new entries, of course, had been beaten to the marketplace by AMC's Gremlin, which returned for 1971 with several improvements, including an exciting new sport trim package called the Gremlin X. With its bucket seats, spearside striping and fat

AMC's Gremlin returned with a host of improvements that included a larger 232-cid six cylinder engine as standard equipment, a new optional 258-cid six, and choice of floor or column mounted shifter at no extra charge.

Hornet got another new model this year, the Sportabout station wagon, which combined the smart styling of a sedan with the usefulness of a compact wagon.

American Motors had a completely redesigned Javelin this year. The unique design included bulging fenders that emphasized the wheels and tires. Inset photo shows racing legend Mark Donahue at the wheel of his Javelin racer.

Top of the new Javelin line was this four passenger Javelin AMX which used the same body as the regular Javelin but featured a unique grille.

AMC's Ambassador got a beautiful new grille this year, as well as standard air conditioning—the only American car with a/c standard on all models.

Copping the award for Best Picture this year was 'The French Connection' starring Gene Hackman as police detective Popeye Doyle. The movie featured one of the most heart-stopping car chases ever filmed.

D70 x 14 Polyglas tires mounted on slot-style wheels, the Gremlin X represented a new idea—a *sporty* subcompact car. Gremlin's base prices for 1971 were $1899 for the two-seat model and $1999 for the regular four-passenger hatchback—and that was cheap money, even back then. As a matter of fact, American Motors had several new entrees this year, unusual because it had introduced so much new stuff the year before. The Hornet line gained two new models, the most popular being the four-door Sportabout station wagon, an attempt to blend sporty looks with station wagon utility. The idea proved a hit, especially with the ladies, and the Sportabout quickly became a hot seller. The other new Hornet was a pocket rocket dubbed the Hornet SC360. A regular two-door sedan fitted a 360-cid V-8, it offered buyers high performance at an exceptionally low price—just $2,663 base. Also new was the intermediate size Matador, which replaced the old Rebel. The Matador was really only a lengthened and facelifted Rebel, but enjoyed the benefit of a greatly simplified model lineup. There was only one Matador trim level, the list of standard features was pretty good by the standards of the day, and the option list was long enough to allow buyers to individualize their Matadors from economical family cars to track-ready racers. Much bigger news

was the all-new Javelin ponycar and its new stablemate, the Javelin-AMX. Both cars featured larger bodies with boldly flared fenders. The AMX was reduced to simply a trim variation of the Javelin. AMC's Ambassador received an extremely attractive new grille, and air conditioning became standard equipment—the only American car line

1971

Top TV Shows

- All in the Family
- The Flip Wilson Show
- Gunsmoke
- The ABC Movie of the Week
- Sanford and Son
- Mannix
- Adam-12
- The Mary Tyler Moore Show

One of the most beautiful family cars of the 1970's was this LeSabre four-door hardtop. Power was provided by a standard 350-cid V8, with a 455 V8 optional.

A man-sized sporty big car, Buick's new Centurion came with a standard 455-cid V8. The Centurion line included this two door hardtop, a four door hardtop plus a convertible.

with air conditioning standard on all models.

Buick's Le Sabre was all new for 1971 and was surely one of the handsomest family cars on the road. Offered in an array of body styles that included two- and four-door hardtops, four-door sedans and a convertible, the big Buick was a solid value. The Wildcat series was gone, replaced by the powerful new Centurion series. Centurions came in either two- or four-door hardtop form, or as a sleek convertible. Buick's huge Electra 225 was also restyled this year, with a larger body and more refined exterior trim. But the biggest sensation that year was the boldly styled Buick Riviera.

Completely new, the Riviera boasted boat-tail rear styling reminiscent of expensive cars of the Classic era. A large fastback rear window swept down to a tapering tail, creating a look that was both rich and sporty. Large wheel openings and crisp character lines made this one of the best styled cars of the decade—and it's still as beautiful and exciting today as it was then. Despite their over-$5,000 sticker price, more than 30,000 of these luxury sport coupes were produced.

Speaking of luxury, Cadillac redesigned its lineup for 1971, with its Calais, De Ville and Fleetwood series showing new, more elegant styling. The flag-ship Eldorado continued to offer a huge 500 cubic

1971
Sports Highlights

- Milwaukee Bucks defeat the Baltimore Bullets, winning four games to the Bullets' zero.

- The Pittsburgh Pirates beat the Baltimore Orioles, four games to threee. (Not a great year for Baltimore fans.)

- In Super Bowl VI, the Dallas Cowboys bounce back this year to defeat the Miami Dolphins, 24-3.

- Al Unser wins yet another Indy 500.

- In tennis, Stan Smith wins the U.S. Open title in September.

inch V-8, and added a beautiful convertible model.

Chevy's Nova didn't look very different from the year before, and it wasn't. However, one major change was that it no longer offered a four-cylinder model. Never a good seller, the four-cylinder Nova's role as an import fighter was taken over by the new

Certainly one of the most distinctive American cars of all time was Buick's fabulous boat-tailed 1971 Riviera Sport Coupe. The beautiful fastback styling made this car a stand-out in the market.

Cadillac re-styled it's line-up this year. Design features included a bold new frontal appearance, stand-up hood ornament and plush interior.

Coupe De Ville was one reason for Cadillac's domination of the luxury car market. Beautiful styling, great engineering and first-rate quality throughout were hallmarks of Cadillac leadership.

Eldorado convertible and Sedan De Ville were two more popular models in Cadillac's hot-selling line-up.

Vega. Camaro showed little outward change, but it had been entirely new the previous year, so not much change could be expected. But Chevy's big cars—the Biscayne, Bel Air, Impala and Caprice—were all new and exceptionally good-looking. Larger, more massive in appearance, and sporting grilles with a hint of Cadillac style, they were family cars that anyone would be proud to own. Over half a million American buyers agreed. Chevy's Corvette offered two models that year—a sport coupe priced at $5,536 and a convertible at a bargain $5,299.

Among the lesser independents, Checker returned for 1971, of course with little change to its taxi and civilian models. As noted, King Midget had expired, but Avanti and Excalibur, two specialty luxury makes, were thriving.

Chrysler brought back the Royal nameplate for 1971—as a budget-priced model of the Newport series. Also returning was the 300 series, which was in decline. There was no letter suffix for the 300, and its 335-horsepower, 440-cube engine wasn't quite the hauler the previous year's 375-horsepower 300H had been.

The Imperial line was cut to a single series, the higher-priced LeBaron. The Crown series was dropped.

Dodge sold a version of the Plymouth Duster coupe, and called it the Demon. Base engine for

both the Demon and Dart line was Chrysler's 198-cid Slant Six—an engine admired to the point of worship by its adherents. Relatively simple and as reliable as an anvil, the Slant Six was legendary for its ability to run forever. A hot version of the car was called the Demon 340—for the 340-cube-inch V-8 it came equipped with. Dodge's mid-size Coronet series was completely restyled, to separate it further from the Charger line. The Coronet now rode a 118-inch wheelbase, while the restyled Chargers came on a 115-inch wheelbase.

Both Dodge and Plymouth joined the subcompact marketing wars this year. However, since Chrysler had been caught napping product-wise,

1971
Top Movies

- Fiddler on the Roof
- Billy Jack
- The French Connection
- Summer of '42
- Diamonds Are Forever.

Chevrolet's answer to increasingly popular import cars was the long-rumored Vega. At it's announcement it was considered an engineering triumph- but unusual design features, especially it's aluminum block engine, proved troublesome, and the Vega's image was soon damaged. Three passenger-car models, plus one sedan delivery model, were offered. Shown here is the handsome Vega hatchback model.

The lowest priced Vega was this two-door sedan. Vega's styling showed a distinct Italian influence.

Also available was the Vega station wagon. Despite it's small size, this highest-priced Vega was a good seller.

the two divisions had to offer imported cars re-badged for sale in the US. Dodge took the smartest route, offering a sturdy little machine called the Dodge Colt. It was built in Japan by Mitsubishi Motors, which did not yet sell cars under it own name in America. The Colt offered a choice of three two-door models—sedan, hardtop and a wagon, plus a neat little four-door sedan, with prices beginning as low as $1,924. Although Japanese quality was not yet as settled in the American mindset as it would later become, in fact the quality was quite good and these Dodge Colts acquitted themselves very well in the market. It was another story, however, with Plymouth's new small car, the Cricket. The builder of the Cricket was Chrysler's British affiliate, Hillman, and the car was an unhappy combination of cheap materials and slap-dash English assembly. Available in a single four-door model priced at $1,915, the Plymouth Cricket soon earned a reputation for being troublesome.

Jeep had a bit of news for 1971. The CJ-5 Renegade II followed in the footsteps (or should I say tire tracks?) of the previous year's Renegade I. The Renegade II came with beautiful cast aluminum wheels, which only added to its sporty appearance. A special Hurst/Jeepster was offered, too. Prepared by Hurst Performance, the Hurst Jeepster featured a hood-mounted tach, rally stripes, and a Hurst

shifter. The Jeepster line included another new specialty model, the limited edition SC-1, which featured special striping.

International Harvester's line of light trucks included the Travelall wagons, handsome pickups, and the Scout line of sport utility vehicles.

Although Ford's big news was the Pinto, the rest of the Ford line had plenty to offer. The full-size Fords were completely new, with Lincolnesque styling that was very attractive. Big Fords came in a range of trim levels including Custom, Custom 500, Galaxie 500, and LTD. In mid-size cars, the Fairlane was dropped, and the Torino soldiered on as Ford's intermediate car line. Two hot new models in the compact Maverick line were the four-door sedan, priced at $2,235, and the sporty new Grabber at $2,354 base. Big news for ponycar enthusiasts was an all-new Mustang. The new model was bigger—over two inches longer and much heavier looking. Sadly, the Boss 302 and Boss 429s were no longer available.

Over at Mercury, the old Comet name returned, as a compact. Comets were badge-engineered versions of the Maverick, and the lineup included two- and four-door models, just like its Maverick stablemate. Cougar received a new look for the front end, heavier and more elegant.

At Pontiac, the emphasis for 1971 was on its big Catalina and Bonneville series, and a new top-of-the-line series, the Grand Ville. Pontiac's look this year was massive but sporty—a big car for men who liked to drive.

Plymouth had really big news for 1971. The Satellite featured all-new "fuselage" styling, a smoother, more integrated look. Two-door and four-door models no longer shared wheelbases (four-doors were two inches longer than the two-doors' 115 inches). The Satellite was a popular fleet car too, and the four-door sedan quickly became America's most recognizable police car.

The world moved on, as it always does. The vivacious Phyllis George became the new Miss America that year, President Nixon escorted his daughter, Tricia, down the aisle at her June wedding, and the Baltimore Colts won the Super Bowl, beating the Cowboys 16-13. In the world of music, Carole King was on top with her hit single "It's Too Late" named Record of the Year; *Tapestry* won Album of the Year, and "You've Got A Friend" was chosen as Song of the Year. Other big songs that year were "A Natural Man" by Lou Rawls, "Proud Mary" by Ike and Tina Turner, and the hilarious "When You're Hot, You're Hot" by Jerry Reed. Winning the Best Picture award that year was *The French Connection*, a cop film starring Gene Hackman, which featured a riveting chase scene.

1971
Music News

- "Satchmo," otherwise known as Louis Armstrong, died on July 6.
- The Jaycees award Elvis Presley as one of America's "10 Outstanding Young Men."
- The Beatles make it official—they're going seperate ways.
- As part of the trend, Simon and Garfunkel also announce they will pursue seperate careers.

Motor Trend named Chevy's Vega "Car of the Year,", perhaps not the best choice when one views the decision with the clarity of hindsight, but altogether not a surprising pick. The choice, however, of a four-cylinder subcompact, a product type that would have been laughed out of the showrooms ten years earlier, as car of the year was certainly a sign that the auto market itself was changing.

Interesting comparison, produced by Chevrolet, shows the differences in size between Chevy's smallest two-door offering, the Vega, and it's largest, the Impala coupe. Note the Vega is more than 46 inches shorter bumper to bumper than the Impala.

Given a choice, we would have preferred this gorgeous Corvette convertible over a Vega any day of the week. The coolest people always equipped their cars with the new 8-track tape players that were just appearing on the market.

Pinto was just 163 inches long, 69.1 inches wide and only 50 inches high. Ford said the styling of the Pinto two door sedan suggested a sporty hardtop. Gas mileage of more than 25 mpg was claimed.

There was little change in the Camaro for 1971- but then again why change a good thing? How many readers out there wish they owned a SS 396 Camaro like this one?

When all was said and done, Chevrolet was still the top producer of big cars, illustrated here in the good-looking Caprice Coupe.

TAILGATE window moves upward into roof cavity . . .   tailgate moves downward into recess in load floor

1971 KINGSWOOD ESTATE "HIDEAWAY" tailgate and rear window in open position

Talk about bold new ideas! The so-called hideaway tailgate and rear window on the Chevrolet Kingswood station wagon opened like a clamshell. The top half disappeared into the roof while the bottom half slid under into a recess in the load floor, leaving the rear area completely open for easier loading. This is one of those unusual features that car collectors find so interesting. Chevy built many thousands of them—where are they today?

New Chrysler Royal was a lower-price model aimed at attracting new buyers to the Chrysler brand.

Dodge got a version of the Plymouth Duster coupe and called it the Demon. Two six cylinder engines and a small V8 used regular gasoline.

A screamin' Demon was this potent Demon 340, powered by a 340-cube V8.

Dodge Dart Swinger continued to offer excellent value with good styling.

Buyers looking for a sporty mid-size Dodge two-door in 1971 had a wide choice. There were a total of six Charger models including the three shown here. Left to right they are the Charger 500, Charger SE and Charger Super Bee.

Dodge's mid-size four door offering was the popular Coronet series.

Oh, to have this in your garage today - a 1971 Dodge Charger R/T! America's favorite straight shooter, John Wayne, talked about his fight with cancer in this ad for the American Cancer Society.

Pert little Dodge Colt bowed this year. Built by Mitsubishi, the neat little Colt was offered in three models-- a four door sedan, station wagon, and a two-door hardtop.

Ford's new little car was dubbed the Pinto, a name most people would remember once they saw this press photo.

Pinto even showed up on the track! Here, racing legend Mickey Thompson is shown with his Pinto Funny car.

Ford Maverick debuted a sporty new Grabber two-door this year.

Mustang was restyled for 1971 and looked much larger than before. The roof-line of the Mustang Sportsroof was particularly interesting.

But for our taste, it's hard to beat the looks of a Mustang convertible. Inset photo shows instrument panel.

Ford Club Wagon was a very popular people mover in this era before mini-vans.

Women's Liberation was a popular theme throughout the country during the 1970's but Honda suggested men could use a bit of liberating too—on a Honda motorcycle, of course.

Big, comfy and quiet would be a good way to describe Ford's LTD for 1971. New front styling was featured.

Ford Ranchero delivered the goods, and came in plain or fancy models- including this GT.

GMC's Sprint, introduced this year, was a good sporty competitor for Ranchero, while Jimmy was a popular SUV

No one had to be told that Lincoln was a BIG car—it's slab-sided styling emphasized it's length and width.

Mercury re-entered the compact market with the new Comet. A badge-engineered version of Ford's Maverick, it was offered in three models in two series—a base two-door sedan and a four-door sedan, plus a special Comet GT coupe.

Mercury's Cougar was a beautifully styled car for folks who wanted a sporty car with a bit more luxury than Mustang could provide.

Olds Delta 88 was completely new in appearance for 1971. Custom coupe shows the graceful new styling, accented by graceful body curves and flush mounted glass.

Oldsmobile was one of America's favorite family cars and it's station wagon models were particularly popular. The Olds Vista Cruiser shown in the foreground here had a unique roofline with windows set into the top and sides of the roof panel. Olds referred to the Vista Cruiser as an 11 window design. The Cutlass Cruiser wagon shown in the background was a less expensive alternative to the flashy Vista Cruiser.

Olds's big luxury two-door was the 98 Coupe, a stylish upper-class statement.

Plymouth's Satellite series included this sharp-looking Satellite Sebring Plus two-door hardtop.

One of the better selling mid-size cars this year was the Satellite four-door sedan—a hit with families and fleets. Note that two- and four-door Satellites used altogether different bodies.

Plymouth Road Runner was appealing to Muscle Heads everywhere, featured standard 383-cid V8 and optional 440 V8 with six-barrel carburetor, or an awesome 426 Hemi V8.

Although kids knew Pontiac for it's muscle cars and flashy Firebird, adults were more likely to buy one of Pontiac's big cars—like this handsome Catalina two-door hardtop. Standard power was a 250-hp 350-cid V8 - and optional engines included a 455-cid V8!

One unfortunate mistake by Plymouth was the Cricket, imported from England. Problem plagued from the start, the little Cricket didn't last long on the market.

More in tune with mainstream America was the big Plymouth Fury, a full-size car with Torsion-Quiet Ride and new front & rear styling.

Elegant Bonneville four door hardtop appealed to families who liked to travel in style and comfort with a bit of sporty-flavor thrown in for good measure.

America's favorite rumpled TV detective, Lt. Columbo, was an affirmed Peugeot enthusiast and his car appeared often on the show.

Chapter Three

1972

V-8s Rule!

Social issues were at the forefront in 1972, and they were reflected in the popular music of the day. George Harrison's *Concert for Bangla Desh* addressed the human misery and starvation facing that tiny country, while Helen Reddy's "I Am Woman" became the rallying song for feminists everywhere.

Richard Nixon was still in the White House, though an event that would have repercussions of historic magnitude occurred in June, when five men were arrested for breaking into the headquarters of the Democratic National Committee. The break-in occurred in a large, gaudy structure in Washington known as the Watergate building, a place that most Americans had not yet heard of,

but which was destined to be burned forever into the American consciousness.

Also becoming part of America's collective memory was the winner of that year's Best Picture award, *The Godfather*, a gangster flick that introduced a new phrase into the national vocabulary, the famous "I'll make him an offer he can't refuse."

"All in the Family" was easily the most popular show on TV, but "Sanford and Son", "Hawaii Five-0," and "Adam-12" were also well-loved. And Laurel Schaefer of Bexley, Ohio was crowned Miss America at that year's pageant in Atlantic City, New Jersey.

Motor Trend magazine shocked many people that year when it named a foreign model as its Car

AMC's Gremlin offered three engine choices this year: a 3.8-liter (232-cid) six, a 4.2-liter (258-cid) six, or a potent 5.0-liter (304-cid) V8, making it the most powerful subcompact economy car on the market.

Popular Gremlin options were the Gremlin X package (a sport appearance group), and the folding fabric sunroof.

Putting the Sport into sport utility was the powerful Jeep CJ-5 Renegade, with a standard 304 V8. Sports enthusiasts could watch pro football now on the new Zenith Super Cromacolor, a futuristic-looking console-type color TV set.

Two great companions for the road—Holiday Inn and a big Buick. Buick's exciting new boat-tailed Riviera met with mixed reaction from buyers. Its radical styling turned off many shoppers.

A very popular and classy mid-size car this year was Buick's handsome Skylark Custom 4-door hardtop.

of the Year. Its choice? The masterful, if temperamental, Citroen SM from France. A Gallic jewel of innovation, the SM featured high-tech engineering matched with a potent Maserati-designed engine.

Yet, despite the bestowing of America's best-known automotive award to a six-cylinder import, and despite too, the previous year's introduction of subcompact cars from America's two biggest brands, the fact remains that the best selling cars for 1972 were the traditional ones—big, V-8-powered sedans, station wagons and coupes.

Lincoln was a good case in point. Ford's luxury division unveiled an all-new Continental Mark IV to replace the much-admired Mark III. The new Mark was more of everything—longer, lower, and sleeker, with more interior room and more luxury. The other Lincolns, the Continental hardtop and sedan, offered only detail improvements. As before, the big Lincolns were powered by a whopper of an engine—460 cubic inches of American-made, cast-iron V-8 muscle.

Even Jeep CJs could be had with V-8 power this year. American Motors lengthened the front end of the ever-popular CJ-5 to provide its range of modern six-cylinder and V-8 engines enough room to fit. All Renegades got the 304 V-8 as standard equipment, while the regular models got a 232-cid six as standard. However, a 258 six and the 304 V-8 could be ordered on any regular CJ-5.

1972
Top News Items

- President Nixon visits China, being the first U.S. leader to travel to the Communist nation. Later in the year, Nixon traveled to Moscow, meeting with Soviet Premier Leonid Brezhnev.

- Apollo 16 completes a successful mission on April 27, and Pioneer 10 journeys to Jupiter, where it will send back photos of the planet and its moons.

- Five men are arrested after breaking in to the Democratic National Headquarters at the Watergate Complex in Washington, D.C.

- Two soon-to-be-big businesses are started this year; Nike, Inc. is founded by Philip Knight and William Bowerman, and Federal Express is founded by Frederick Smith.

Mercury had news, too. Its Montego series added a new GT model, while dropping the old Cyclone series. Montego's styling was undeniably handsome

Buick's Skylark line also included this sporty Skylark Sun Coupe, which featured a folding vinyl sunroof. The sunroof opening measured 42 inches by 50 inches.

Big cars were the most popular models in America this year, and Buick had a complete line of offerings. This LeSabre four-door hardtop was among the most coveted family cars on the road. For 1972, it received a distinctive new die-cast grille. All LeSabres ordered with the 350-cid V-8 came with a new three-speed Turbo-Hydra-matic 375-B transmission, while those equipped with the larger 455-cubic-inch engine came with the Turbo-Hydra-matic 400.

Immensely popular with the upper crust was this Cadillac Coupe DeVille, which for 1972 included a new impact resisting bumper system. The Allstate Insurance Company was advertising the advantages of air bags—though none were yet on the market.

Another popular Cadillac was the Sedan DeVille, a big, comfortable four-door hardtop sedan.

Big cars were known to be safer than small cars, and they didn't get much bigger than this—the Cadillac Fleetwood Sixty Special Brougham.

Another big car was the Chrysler Newport Royal, shown here in two-door hardtop guise.

this year—its luxurious grille was styled along the same lines as the sporty Cougar. Montego four-doors were now pillared hardtops, rather than the traditional sedans. The Comet and Cougar lines saw only detail changes, while the big Mercs offered radial tires for the first time, along with Sure-Track, an anti-skid brake system pioneered by Ford.

Oldsmobile's model lineup started at the F-85 intermediate, priced at $2,837 for a basic V-8 town sedan. From there, the line rose through the Cutlass and Cutlass Supreme series, up to the Delta Eighty-Eight and Eighty-Eight Royale big cars, the massive Ninety-Eights, and topped out with the Toronado coupe, stickered at $5,341. The full-size Oldsmobiles offered a new safety bumper system that protected the car in crashes up to 2.5 mph—quite a feat in those days, as bumpers had long since become more ornamental than protective.

To compete with Cadillac and Lincoln, Chrysler offered this elegant New Yorker Brougham, a plush four door hardtop. TV and radio personality Arthur Godfrey was a Chrysler spokesman.

Three views of Chevy's beautiful Camaro—the regular Sport Coupe (top) and the SS Coupe (middle and lower photos).

Chevrolet sold a great many Chevelle Malibu Sport Coupes in 1972, and for good reason—it was a good-looking car of exceptional value.

The full-size Chevy line included Impala and Caprice models, each with its own unique grille.

Shoppers looking for a low-priced, full-size Dodge probably would've chosen the Dodge Polara. Built on a 122-inch wheelbase, the big Dodge had a 318-cid V8 as standard equipment.

Pontiac's lineup, unlike Oldsmobile's, began with a compact car, the budget-priced Ventura II, priced at $2,312 for a stripped coupe. Introduced in mid-1971, the Ventura was more or less a Chevy Nova with a Pontiac grille and trim. One magazine noted that, although Pontiac's ad theme that year was "Pure Pontiac," the Ventura "is almost pure unadulterated Chevrolet." However, the smallest Pontiac did offer an interesting option package—the Sprint included sport appearance items, and was a very attractive package. Ventura buyers could order either a 250-cid six or a 307 V-8, both produced by Chevy. Pontiac's Firebird saw only detail changes for 1972, most noticeable of which was the Endura front end, an energy absorbing material, color-matched to the body.

Pontiac was still pushing its well-earned performance image, and the Firebird Trans Am offered a 300-horsepower, 455-cid V-8, while the GTO returned as an option package on the LeMans. Muscle cars like the GTO were being hurt by high auto insurance premiums and their popularity was declining. Even so, the Pontiac offered a regular production Grand Prix SJ with a 455-cubic-inch V-8, as well as the limited production Hurst Grand Prix SSJ, offered at $5,619.

Over at Plymouth, the Valiant sedans received redesigned seats and improved TorqueFlite transmissions. The Barracuda coupe returned in two models, but its convertible stablemate had been dropped. Base Barracudas came with a 225-cube Slant Six as standard, V-8 optional, while the performance-oriented 'Cuda models got a 4 bbl 340-cube V-8 as standard. An electric sunroof was a new option. Satellites continued to be offered in two distinct shapes—one for two-door hardtops, one for sedans and wagons. The big Fury received wider axles.

1972
Top Tv Shows

- All in the Family
- Sanford and Son
- Hawaii Five-O
- Maude
- Bridget Loves Bernie
- The NBC Sunday Mystery Movie
- The Mary Tyler Moore Show
- Gunsmoke
- The Wonderful World of Disney
- Ironside

Dodge buyers looking for something a bit more luxurious than the Polara would've gone ape over this Monaco hardtop.

Dodge's mid-size line-up came with two nameplates this year. Two-doors were marketed as Dodge Chargers.

The four-door, mid-size Dodge sedans were tagged as Coronets.

American Motors didn't have much new in the way of models, but bragged about quality improvements across their entire car line. Coupled with the improved quality was a new best-in-the-industry warranty program dubbed the Buyer Protection Plan (BPP). With it, customers were guaranteed a free loaner car if warranty repairs required leaving the car more than a day. The BPP proved to be a great marketing tool, and consumer confidence in AMC products rose sharply. Other AMC news included the addition of a V-8 option for the little Gremlin, turning the erstwhile economy champ into a mini-muscle car. The Hornet line no longer offered the rampaging SC360 model, but happily most of the equipment, including the 360-cid V-8, was still optionally available. AMC decided to drop all its base models for 1972—even its bargain-priced Gremlin two-passenger model. The base Gremlin now was a four-seater, priced at $1,999. The Hornet base series was also dropped, leaving only the high-line SST models.

The Skylark 350 returned to the Buick Skylark range for 1972, after a one-year absence. A new Sun Coupe option, which included a sunroof, was available. The whole range of Buick intermediates impressed auto writers with their smart styling and feel of quality.

Chevrolet was the volume leader in cars back then and the reasons for its leading position were obvious. With the hot-selling Vega, the compact Nova, the beautiful Camaro, the style-setting Monte Carlo, the Malibu and Chevelle intermediates, on up to the big Chevrolet full-size models—plus America's only true sport car—Chevy had a car for every need or desire, and they all were selling well.

Chevy's big car range included the base-line Biscayne and Bel Air series, which came only as four-door sedans. However, these appealed almost exclusively to fleet buyers—government, police, taxi companies and utility companies. The better-trimmed Impala series, and the plush (well, by Chevy standards, anyway) Caprice accounted for the bulk of retail orders. The compact Nova line showed detail improvements only, and curiously enough, still offered the old-fashioned two-speed Powerglide automatic transmission, though only with the standard six engine. For a bit more cash, a wise shopper could specify the much more modern Turbo Hydra-matic. Chevy's beautiful Camaro got a new standard grille with a large grid pattern, and the four spoke steering wheel became standard equipment.

Over at Dodge, the Dart series introduced new safety items including three-point seat belts and larger tail lamps, as well as minor changes to the grille. The Challenger sported a new optional sun-

1972

Sports Highlights

- The Los Angeles Lakers pummel the New York Knicks, 4 games to 1.

- In the World Series, the Oakland A's beat the Cincinnati Reds 4 games to 3.

- The Miami Dolphins come back swimming; they defeat the Washington Redskins 14-7 in Super Bowl VII.

roof, electrically operated no less, to replace the convertible models that were no longer offered. Only two Challengers were offered; a base coupe, available with either a six or V-8; and the Rallye, offered only as a V-8 coupe. As before, Dodge intermediates carried two names—four-door sedans and station wagons wore Coronet badges, while the two-doors went by the name of the Charger. Chargers were mechanically similar to the Coronets, but had a shorter wheelbase and unique styling. At the top of the Charger line was the SE, which had a more formal roof treatment than the rest of the Charger line.

1972

Top Movies

- The Godfather
- The Poseidon Adventure
- What's Up Doc?
- Deliverance
- Jeremiah Johnson

The big Dodges—the Polara, and up the price scale a bit, the Monaco—featured new looks for 1972. Previously, the only differences between the two series were trim variations. This year, however, each had unique styling. Polara had a low-set grille with quad headlamps inset, while Monaco's front end styling was more elegant, with concealed headlamps mounted above the bumper.

Ford's small car lineup for 1972 featured the popular Pinto, back with some minor improvements, and the Maverick, smallest of the American compact cars. Mavericks could be ordered with radial ply tires for the first time, as well as an AM-FM monaural radio. Mustang returned relatively unchanged—but after all, it had been all new for 1971. Three body styles were available—hardtop, Sportsroof and convertible. One mid-season change was the addition of a seatbelt warning buzzer, a harbinger of things to come.

Ford's Torino series, one of the best-selling mid-size cars of the decade, was all new for 1972. The Torino was designed to give more of the "big car" feel that Americans loved. Torinos reverted to a separate frame and body design and featured new front and rear suspensions, including the luxury of coil springs at all four wheels. Four body styles were offered—a two-door hardtop, a two-door Sportsroof, a four-door pillared hardtop, and a four-door station wagon.

Any young lady would have loved to own this beautiful Dodge Challenger coupe—it was good for trips to the beach or for burning rubber.

Ford's sporty personal car, the Thunderbird, was also all-new, and like the Torino, featured body-on-frame construction. The wheelbase was increased by six inches, overall length by four inches, making this one big 'bird indeed. Only one style, a two-door hardtop, was offered, and it came standard with a 400-cid V-8 engine, with a 429 V-8 optional. Standard tires were steel belted radials. Ford's popular big car line offered a wide range of models in Ford Custom, Custom 500, Galaxie 500 and LTD variations. The Custom and Custom 500s were strictly low-budget cars, offered mainly to fleet users, and came only as four-door sedans and wagons. The Galaxie 500 series added two- and four-door hardtops to the mix, while the top-line LTD also included a four-door pillared hardtop and a two-door convertible.

The Chrysler brand for 1972 continued to offer what the customers wanted—big cars. Their autos

had a new look this year. The Chrysler Newports featured cleanly styled grilles and massive-looking bodies with smooth flanks. Starting at around $4,000, the Newport line was a reasonably priced entry into luxury car ownership. The upscale New Yorker's grille was more stylized. Like most American big cars of the time, the Chryslers came with mammoth V-8 engines, either 400-cid or 440-cid, depending on the model.

It wasn't such a mystery, the reason why American cars had become so big. America is a huge country, with its vast distances bridged by probably the best highway system on earth—and Americans love to drive. Cars naturally became bigger to provide the room and comfort people needed when traveling those great distances. Hand in hand with the increased car size was the need for bigger and bigger engines to haul all that mass. And anyway, Americans love speed and power—always have, probably always will. It's in our blood.

So, V-8 engines were the standard of the day and six-cylinder engines were an also-ran. Four-cylinder cars were still mainly reserved for the fringe element, the eccentric people among us who try to protect the environment, promote peace or become automotive writers.

Business was good in 1972 and V-8s clearly ruled the market. But cosmic forces were at work and changes were coming. It wasn't visible at all in 1972, and hints of it wouldn't appear until late the following year. When that change came, it would cause a panic in the market. But before all that came about, the American auto industry would enjoy one of the greatest years in its history.

The 1972 Thunderbird.

Redesigned from the inside out. Precise in its handling, superlative in its ride. A magnificent new personal automobile.

Personal in its luxurious appointments as well. In its distinctive trim, its thick cut pile carpeting. Its power front disc brakes and power steering. And these are only part of this remarkable automobile's standard equipment. It's personal, too, in its options. For example, an electronic anti-skid brake system and the split bench seat, the vinyl roof, the whitewalls and the deluxe wheel covers pictured above. Don't you owe yourself a personal encounter with this magnificent new Thunderbird? At your Ford Dealer's.

THUNDERBIRD

FORD DIVISION (Ford)

Ford's Thunderbird had certainly grown larger over the years, and now was Lincoln-size.

The less you spend on a car, the more you can spend on other things.

This car gets up to 40 miles to the gallon
Up to 75 miles an hour
Overhead cam engine, rack and pinion steering, 4-speed synchromesh transmission, power-assisted front disc brakes, front bucket seats, radial tires, tachometer, racing mirror. All standard equipment.
Oh, it doesn't have automatic transmission, air conditioning, and a 400-horsepower engine.
But which would you rather have? Automatic transmission, air conditioning, and a 400-horsepower engine?
Or Michelle and Tammy and Alison?

The Honda Coupe. $1735.
It makes a lot of sense.

A new nameplate in the import car market was Honda, long known as a producer of high quality motorcycles and motor scooters. Honda's new 600 Coupe was priced at an amazingly low $1735—and Honda had a two-door sedan that was even less expensive.

Two views of the Plymouth Barracuda ponycar show just how attractive a car it was.

Mercury Capri, imported from Ford of Germany, gave decent performance with its standard four-cylinder engine. In size, the Capri reminded some of the original Ford Mustang.

Mercury Montego was one of the most popular mid-sized cars, and the Mary Tyler Moore show was one of America's favorite TV programs.

Big cars were hot this year, and the Olds 98 was one of the better ones.

Huge luxury coupes like the Toronado were popular among youngish executives.

Also popular among families was the inexpensive mid-sized Satellite from Plymouth, which became perhaps the most recognizable police car of the decade.

Plymouth's imported Cricket line added this new four-door station wagon this year.

Motor Trend magazine named the Citroen SM "Car of the Year"—certainly a surprising choice in a year when so many buyers showed a preference for American iron.

A really cool car this year was Pontiac's Ventura II with the Sprint option. Sprint's standard equipment included a three-speed manual floor shift, special identification, custom steering wheel, wheel trim rings, custom carpets, black textured grille and special side striping. A 250-cid six was standard, and a folding vinyl sunroof was optional.

Pontiac's 1972 Grand Prix had a new grille protected by a massive bumper. Grand Prix this year came standard with a 400-cid V8 and Hydra-matic. A 455-cid V8 was optional on the model J and standard on the SSJ.

Top of the popular LeMans line was the Luxury LeMans, available in two- and four-door hardtop models.

The aggressive-looking Firebird Formula combined sleek styling and top performance and was the object of desire by many a young man that year. Firebird Formula was offered as a 350, 400 or a 455, depending on engine, and was easily recognized by the fiberglass hood with dual air scoops. Pontiac's Firebird was also offered in standard, Esprit and Trans Am models.

Chapter Four

1973

It Was A Very Good Year

At the opening of the 1973 model year, prosperity reigned throughout America. Auto industry sales for the previous year had been good, and the outlook was for even greater car sales. Overall, the economy was humming along sweetly and the country was in a happy frame of mind.

In January of 1973, a cease-fire agreement was reached, signaling the end of America's military action in Vietnam. The South Vietnamese army would thereafter be responsible for keeping the country out of the grips of Communism.

It was a good year for movies. One of the most popular films of the decade, *American Graffiti*, was packing the theaters. Its novel theme of nostalgia soon launched a string of retrospective movies, none of which managed to capture the fun of the original. Also in theaters was the horror film *The Exorcist*, based on the popular novel. But capturing the Oscar

for Best Picture that year was the wonderful Paul Newman-Robert Redford buddy picture, *The Sting*, a light-hearted look at con men in the 1930s. However, as good as both Newman and Redford were, the award for Best Actor went to Jack Lemmon, for his excellent performance in the role of a middle-aged businessman whose life is falling apart in *Save the Tiger*. Another great film was the little-remembered romance *A Touch of Class*, which earned Glenda Jackson an Academy Award for Best Actress.

The Record of the Year was Roberta Flack's "Killing me Softly," which somehow managed to outscore Gladys Knight and the Pips' soulful "Midnight Train to Georgia." On television, "All in the Family" continued its reign as the top rated show, followed by "The Waltons" and "Sanford & Son".

And pretty Terry Meeuwsen of De Pere, Wisconsin was crowned as the new Miss America.

Still in the lineup was AMC's big car, the Ambassador. Offered as a hardtop coupe, shown, or as a traditional four-door sedan, Ambassador was a plush, quiet road cruiser that should have sold better than it did.

We Won!
Now you win with the
Trans Am* Victory Javelin

For the second year in a row, specially prepared and modified Javelins beat all the other hot cars in the Trans American Racing Series and we feel like celebrating.

We won the championship, and now with the specially equipped Trans Am Victory Javelin, you get 14" slot style wheels, E-70 x 14 white lettered wide polyglas tires, space-saver spare tire and a Trans Am winner medallion on the side panel at no extra charge.

We call it the Trans Am Victory Package. American Motors includes this special equipment listing for $167.45 at no cost.

And remember, only American Motors makes this promise: The Buyer Protection Plan backs every '73 car we build and we'll see that our dealers back that promise.

So come see the winner at your American Motors dealer and find out why we say: We back them better because we build them better.

George Follmer/ Roy Woods/ Trans-Am Racing Team

Manufacturer's suggested retail price of the specially equipped Trans Am Victory Javelin is $2939.00. State and local taxes not included, destination charges and other options extra.
*SCCA Inc. is the proprietor of the marks "Trans Am" and "SCCA."

Buckle up for safety.

AMC /▮ Javelin
We back them better because we build them better.

AMERICAN MOTORS BUYER PROTECTION PLAN /▮
1. A simple, strong guarantee, just 101 words! When you buy a new 1973 car from an American Motors dealer, American Motors Corporation guarantees to you that, except for tires, it will pay for the repair or replacement of any part it supplies that is defective in material or workmanship. This guarantee is good for 12 months from the date the car is first used or 12,000 miles, whichever comes first. All we require is that the car be properly maintained and cared for under normal use and service in the fifty United States or Canada, and that guaranteed repairs or replacement be made by an American Motors dealer.
2. A free loaner car from almost every one of our dealers if guaranteed repairs take overnight.
3. Special Trip Interruption Protection.
4. And a toll free hot line to AMC Headquarters.

AMC was flying high this year, and celebrated its Trans Am win by introducing this limited edition Trans Am Victory Javelin, equipped with slotted wheels, big tires and Trans Am medallion on the side. George Follmer and Roy Woods appeared in AMC's advertisements for the no-charge package.

"The styling coup of '73"

When we introduced the Hornet Hatchback this fall, Car & Driver Magazine called it "The styling coup of '73."

And along with sportscar styling, you get room to travel in; 23 cubic feet of cargo space with the back seat folded down.

Now we've added something else. An optional Levi's interior. The look of jeans,

copper buttons, orange stitching...even a Levi's tab.

So if you want the style, the performance, the room, the Levi's interior and the American Motors Buyer Protection Plan, get a Hornet Hatchback at your AMC dealer, where he'll give you a good deal and a good deal more.

Buckle up for safety.

AMERICAN MOTORS BUYER PROTECTION PLAN /▮
1. A simple, strong guarantee, just 101 words! When you buy a new 1973 car from an American Motors dealer, American Motors Corporation guarantees to you that, except for tires, it will pay for the repair or replacement of any part it supplies that is defective in material or workmanship. This guarantee is good for 12 months from the date the car is first used or 12,000 miles, whichever comes first. All we require is that the car be properly maintained and cared for under normal use and service in the fifty United States or Canada, and that guaranteed repairs or replacement be made by an American Motors dealer.
2. A free loaner car from almost every one of our dealers if guaranteed repairs take overnight.
3. Special Trip Interruption Protection.
4. And a toll free hot line to AMC Headquarters.

AMC /▮ Hornet
We back them better because we build them better.

Several companies introduced hatchback cars this year, but the best looking one of the bunch was American Motors' Hornet Hatchback, which Car and Driver called "The Styling Coup of '73."

Levi's Gremlin, with seats of the pants

Now a Gremlin with upholstery that's like blue denim Levi's.® Has orange stitching, the buttons, even the famous Levi's tab on both front seats.

Everything else on the car is pure Gremlin. You get the same fun styling. That quiet six cylinder engine. More width and weight than all other little economy cars.

True to the American Motors Buyer Protection Plan, both Gremlin and its Levi's are guaranteed* for one year or 12,000 miles.

Levi's Gremlin. The economy car that wears the pants.

Buckle up for safety.

New on the Gremlin this year was a Levi's seat trim option. Made out of a spun nylon fabric that looked and felt like denim (but unlike denim, would meet federal regulations for fire resistance), the Levi's seats were another way AMC was able to offer something truly unique in the market. Public acceptance was quite good.

As before, Buick dealers offered the line of Opel cars imported from Germany. New this year was a luxury offering, the beautiful Opel Manta Luxus. More luxurious than a Saab or Toyota, but not quite as ritzy as a Mercedes, the new Opel could best be described as a German Buick—and quite appropriate for Buick's U.S. dealers to offer.

Jeep sales were continuing to post solid increases this year. Showing renewed popularity was the Jeep truck, shown here with an available slide-on cab-over camper unit.

There were a few significant evolutionary changes in automotive design. Pontiac Motor Division introduced a car with very unique styling. The new Grand Am was pitched as an American gran turismo, a high-speed tourer like the fanciest European cars. In size, it was what passed for an intermediate-size car back then, meaning it was rather large and bulky, and the styling of its bold front snout was impossible to ignore. Although it wasn't really what the public (or GM, for that matter) was searching for, it was an early advocate of the non-chrome bumper look that has become the norm these days. And it sold fairly well, too.

In the subcompact market, the Datsun 1200 and Toyota Corolla were two big sellers, though the venerable VW Beetle was still the first choice for many. It's hard for people today to comprehend the hold that VW had on the small car market, but from the late 1950s to the mid-1970s, it remained the car to beat. Fiat's stubby little 128 sedan was another small car choice, but the company didn't have as large and far-ranging a service network as Volkswagen's, and that was a real drawback.

A bit up the price scale was the new Datsun 610, a more stylish series, which was introduced to replace the 510 model. However, Datsun kept a simple 510 two-door in its lineup as a price leader. The French automaker Renault offered its new 12 model, introduced in mid-1971, in four-door sedan and station wagon models. Alas, the Renault image wasn't very good in the U.S. back then, and the little 12 failed to attract many buyers.

1973

Top News Items

- The first planeload of POWs return from Vietnam.

- Gasoline rationing begins as the effects of the embargo start to be felt.

- Juan Peron gets another chance as Argentina's president.

- Vice-President Spiro Agnew resigns.

- Direct American involvement with Vietnam ends.

- Pablo Picasso dies at age 91.

Buick's popular Century Luxus was a plush offering in the mid-size market and was an ideal family car.

A very popular mid-size coupe was this handsome Century two-door. Note the elegant sweep of the body lines and the way the fender lines blend into the doors.

People sometimes wonder why big cars were so popular in the 1970's but a look at this magnificent Buick Le Sabre is all the explanation needed. The big Buick was extremely good-looking, fast, comfortable and safe. Kojak, starring Telly Savalas, was a popular TV show.

Among the domestic small cars, AMC's Gremlin was continuing to grow in popularity. Although it lacked the advanced design and extra standard features of the imports, many buyers realized the Gremlin's conventional engineering would likely prove more reliable over the long haul. Ford's Pinto returned for a third year, boasting new colors and a host of new standard features including glove box lock, passenger side courtesy light, and a cigarette lighter—and yes, those items had been optional previously.

Some magazines were beginning to report problems on Chevy's little Vega. The troubles were numerous, but were mostly caused by poor assembly quality, forcing owners to return to dealers many times for adjustments and repairs. Much of it came as a result of labor problems at the Vega factory at Lordstown, Ohio. A young, militant union was protesting what it saw as too much pressure to produce more cars, at excessive line speeds, too much mandatory overtime, poorly planned work speed-ups, and more. Ominously, a separate problem was also appearing. It seemed that the littlest Chevy was experiencing a surprisingly high rate of engine failures.

The balance of the Chevy line had no such troubles. The Nova series added a new hatchback coupe, though its styling, like the other Novas, was based on the same body that Chevy had introduced in 1968. The hatchback was a new concept for American cars and interest in it was all out of pro-

1973

Top TV Shows

- All in the Family
- The Waltons
- Sanford and Son
- M*A*S*H*
- Hawaii Five-O
- Maude
- Kojak
- The Sonny and Cher Comedy Hour
- The Mary Tyler Moore Show
- Cannon

Cadillac was also a hot seller this year, and this Coupe DeVille is a good example of why. Cadillac's bold, elegant styling was cleaner and more contemporary than most, and its cars were instantly identifiable as Cadillacs.

In the early 1970s, Cadillac was the best selling luxury car in the world, and the brand name stood for the best there was in life. Shown is the Sedan DeVille.

portion to actual sales. Novas were available with a 250-cid six or a choice of three V-8s—a 307-cid and a 350-cid that could be had with either two- or four-barrel carburetor. Camaro added an LT (for "lusso turismo," or "luxury touring") model that came with V-8 engine, power steering and fancier trim all standard. Chevy's biggest news for 1973 was its all-new Chevelle series, which included a new Laguna model in addition to the regular Chevelle and Malibu models. All-new "Colonnade hardtop" styling for two-doors debuted, and the rest of the line featured a heavier, more solid look than previous Chevelles. In the full-size Chevy line, the Biscayne series was dropped, leaving the Bel Air as the bottom series. The Caprice was renamed Caprice Classic, and further upgraded to make it even more plush than before.

At Dodge, the Demon was renamed the Dart Sport, joining the Dart Swinger and Dart sedans in Chrysler's very popular compact line. The Challenger series now included as standard equipment electronic ignition and front disc brakes, as well as a number of mechanical improvements. Bigger news came in the Coronet and Charger series, which boasted vastly improved sound deadening, making these cars equal in silence to more expensive automobiles. Both nameplates included the old standby Slant Six engine as standard equipment, though V-8s were the usual choice of buyers. In its big car line, the Polara received new styling, a more conventional look that some felt resembled the full-size Chevrolet. The Dodge Monaco, however, continued the styling theme it had used the previous year.

1973
Sports Highlights

- George Foreman knocks out Joe Frazier to gain the world championship.
- One for the Down Under: Australia wins the Davis Cup.
- Billie Jean King trounces Bobby Riggs in three straight sets.
- In the World Series, the Oakland A's defeat the New York Mets 4 games to 3.
- The Dolphins have another great season, beating the Minnesota Vikings 24-7 in Super Bowl VIII.

At AMC, the big news was a hatchback version of the Hornet. Hatchback cars were rare in the U.S. back then, but several companies were introducing them in 1973. Of the bunch, however, the Hornet was easily the best looking. *Car and Driver* thought so, and called the new Hornet "The Styling Coup of 1973," quite an honor for AMC. The Matador line got a new grille and interior improvements. AMC's lovely Ambassador, which already boasted the most comprehensive list of standard equipment short of a Rolls-Royce, now added power steering, power disc brakes, radio, clock, undercoating, white wall tires and more, to its list of standard features.

Cadillac's Fleetwood Eldorado for 1973 retained the classic good looks of its predecessors but received a new grille, taillights and side moldings. The grille was mounted to the bumper so that it would retract with the bumper on impact—it was hoped this would reduce repair costs.

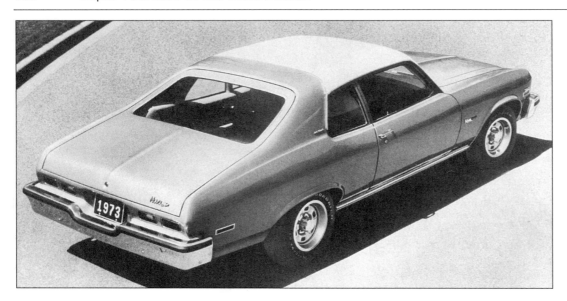

Chevy Nova now offered a hatchback model in addition to its regular two- and four-door sedans. Vega, of course, also offered a hatchback, and for 1973 introduced new colors, including four that were unique to the Vega line.

The 1973 Chrysler Imperial Le Baron four-door hardtop emphasized comfort, safety and luxury.

AMC's Jeep division had little news, but again offered the popular CJ-5 Renegade as a limited production offering.

Ford's lineup of convertible models had dwindled over the years and for 1973 was down to just one—a Mustang priced around $3,100. Mustang's popularity had waned considerably, as had all the ponycars, and most analysts were convinced it was because the formerly compact and youthful cars had become too big. In truth, the ponycars had grown over the years, to the point where they were almost indistinguishable from conventional mid-size hardtops. In fact, many of the ponycars shared components with their bigger stablemates. The full-size Ford line was restyled this year, handsome enough, but some writers complained it resembled too closely the earlier models.

It was a similar story with Mercury's model lineup. The Comet received a host of minor improvements aimed at making it quieter and more refined than before. Cougar now added automatic transmission and power disc brakes to its list of standard features. The popular Montego lineup likewise saw detail changes. The big Mercury models underwent the greatest alteration in 1973, with new sheet metal and new rooflines. The big Mercury Marquis now looked very much like a Lincoln.

In the luxury car class, the three contenders were—as before—Cadillac, Lincoln, and Imperial, in that order. Cadillac was known as the "Standard of the World," Lincoln's Mark series were style leaders, and Imperial was, well, a nice, big car.

Plymouth's hot seller was the Valiant, a compact car that skirted the limits of its category, since it offered nearly as much interior room as some intermediates. The Valiants received styling updates front and rear, and interiors were upgraded a bit. Dusters now offered a fold-down rear seat, and a sunroof. Chrysler referred to models equipped with both options as "Convertriples," since they had some features of a convertible (the sunroof), and some of a station wagon (the fold-down rear seat) in a conventional coupe. Well, okay, it *was* a stretch. The Fury line featured new styling

1973

Top Movies

- The Exorcist
- The Sting
- American Graffiti
- Papillon
- The Way We Were

that was more conventional than the previous year—and we'll say more handsome as well.

Oldsmobile was riding a sales boom in 1973, and extended its line down-market with its new Omega series. Omega was a compact, and even the most casual observer could readily see it was basically a re-badged Chevrolet Nova. With a six-cylinder coupe that began at $2,612, Olds was now nudging the low-priced market. Other styles included a four-door sedan and a hatchback coupe. Oldsmobile's big news, though, was its intermediate Cutlass line, which was completely restyled this year. Bodies were longer and much more elegant. The Cutlass Supreme in particular showed great appeal, with its formal roofline, waterfall grille, and what was to become the most preeminent styling feature of the 1970s—the "opera window." With the new Omega, fancy Cutlass and solid Delta Eighty-Eight (which still included a very handsome convertible model), Oldsmobile sales soared.

The Pontiac Motor Division was nearing a crossroads. Its appeal had been based on its sporty image, with its ponycars and muscle cars being solid favorites for several years. Now, the ponycar market was sinking, and the muscle car era was coming to a close, leaving Pontiac with the need to cultivate a more appropriate (and marketable) image. The division tried

1973
Music News

- Elvis broadcasts his benefit concert from Hawaii via satellite, reaching one and half billion viewers. At the time, it was the most expensive special ever done.

- The Allman Brothers release the hit single "Ramblin' Man." The music style "Country Rock" becomes well established.

- Roberta Flack's song "Killing Me Softly" is released and goes to number one on the charts and wins Record of the Year.

several approaches. Firebirds retained their basic styling, though the Trans Am got a new "chicken" decal for the hood. Ventura added a hatchback coupe to the line, and still offered the sporty Sprint package, and the intermediate line was extended with the addition of the aforementioned Grand Am. The big Pontiacs received new front-end styling, giving them a more luxurious appearance than before.

For 1973, anyone interested in a two-door mid-sized Chevy had several choices, including the family-favorite Chevelle Malibu coupe and the lush Monte Carlo coupe (inset).

The Malibu sedan for 1973 combined good looks with excellent value, and was a top-selling family car. GM's Delco division was promoting its service parts in enthusiast magazines.

That other GM brand, Buick, introduced a new Opel model. Like all Opels sold in American thus far, it was imported from Germany. The new Manta Luxus was an unusual creature—a mid-priced import. Most foreign cars in that decade were either low-priced economy cars, or high priced luxury cars, but this new Opel was much more plush than any econo-box, yet not quite a Mercedes-level offering. It was more or less a German Buick—and the public loved it. Like its sister divisions, Buick offered redesigned mid-sized cars for 1973. The Century and Century Luxus replaced the old Skylark and Skylark Custom. Like other GM intermediates, the new Buicks featured a Colonnade hardtop design, wherein frameless door glass is used in conjunction with conventional sedan roof pillars. This gave some of the feel of true hardtop style, but with the roof strength of a sedan, useful in a rollover accident. Buick's big cars received styling updates.

In October, Vice President Spiro Agnew was compelled to resign from office in disgrace, over allegations he had received kickbacks while serving as Governor of Maryland. He eventually pleaded no contest to a charge of income tax evasion.

All in all, it was a great year for the automotive industry. Chevrolet's Monte Carlo was named *Motor Trend*'s Car of the Year. Sales of passenger cars and light trucks set an all-time record, with 11,222,470 US cars sold, plus 2,735,557 trucks and 1,870,555 imported cars sold. The total, 13,958,027, was more than a million greater than 1972's number—and 1972 had been a very good year. Storm clouds were rising, though, and very soon, small cars and fuel economy were going to become the most popular topics of social conversation in a country that had never thought much about either.

Three handsome two-door Chevys were the Camaro (top); Chevelle Laguna, a new model this year (middle); and the popular Monte Carlo (bottom), Motor Trend magazine's Car of the Year.

The best-selling car in America was the full-size Chevrolet—which offered a very wide range of models, including this handsome Caprice hardtop.

Dodge Polara was re-styled this year, gaining a good-looking new grille. It's a pity no company offers a true four-door pillarless hardtop these days—it's such a beautiful style.

Dodge continued to split its mid-size cars into two brand names. Four-door models were marketed as Coronets, while two-doors went under the Charger name.

Jack Lord starred in the hit TV police show "Hawaii 5-0", while Dodge Dart was a star in the compact car market.

Chrysler Corporation, alone among U.S. car companies, didn't offer an American-built subcompact car, so Dodge dealers were given the Dodge Colt, built in Japan by Mitsubishi, to round out their small car lines. Colt came in four-door sedan and station wagon versions, as well as a good-looking two-door hardtop.

Mustang had grown bigger over the years, while its sales had shrunk, but America's first ponycar still offered a lot of excitement for a reasonable price. Both the convertible and the Mach I fastback are highly prized by collectors today.

The full-sized Fords got new sheet metal below the window line, plus new tail-lamps and impact-absorbing bumpers. New options this year included an anti-theft alarm, radio with 8-track tape player, and power mini-vent windows.

Ford's top-selling LTD also sported a new, segmented grille this year. A 351-2V V-8, Select-Shift Cruise-O-Matic transmission, power steering and power front disc brakes were standard in all the new big Fords.

Ford's low-priced full-sized family car was the Galaxie 500, shown here in four-door, pillared hardtop form. Like all the big Fords this year, the Galaxie received new sheet metal below the window line.

In this decade before minivans, the most-desired family car was the Ford Country Squire station wagon, a full-size behemoth that could swallow up all the kids, suitcases and grocery bags that were thrown into it. Dual-facing rear seats were available for the cargo area, and could even be had with a recreation table that fit between them!

Top of the Ford Motor Company product line was the Lincoln series. Two hot models were the gorgeous Continental Mark IV, new this year, and the Continental four-door.

For 1973, Mercury's Cougar received several design changes, including a new vertical die-cast grille and distinctive four-pod sequential taillights. All 1973 Lincoln-Mercury cars got new damage-resistant front bumper systems designed to prevent significant damage to safety-related components in a 5-mph crash. Cougar XR-7 included a three-quarter vinyl roof.

The styling theme for Mercury's Montego was very similar to the Cougar. Nine models were offered, with two-doors built on a 114-inch wheelbase and four-doors mounting a 118-inch wheelbase.

Mercury's big Marquis Brougham was completely restyled this year, and now resembled the more expensive Lincoln models.

One of the best looking convertibles on the market was the big Delta 88 Royale from Oldsmobile.

Olds was one of the top-selling car lines in America, and the Cutlass Supreme was one reason why. Its combination of good looks and value in a mid-size package had strong appeal to families.

The Cutlass four-door was another strong seller from the red-hot Oldsmobile Division, and was a beautiful and highly functional family car.

Oldsmobile's Cutlass "S" Colonnade Hardtop Coupe used traditional hardtop-style doors with frameless window glass on a pillared coupe, creating a style known as the Colonnade Hardtop. It was believed to be safer than a regular hardtop in a rollover accident, but lacked the hardtop's wide-open appeal. Nonetheless, this was a strong seller for Olds.

America's oldest car division entered the compact car market in 1973 with the Olds Omega, which came as a two-door coupe, a hatchback coupe, or a four-door sedan. It was obvious to most buyers that the Omega was a badge-engineered version of Chevy's Nova.

Plymouth offered a full range of cars this year, including this big Fury Gran Coupe. Note the stand-up hood ornament, which would soon become one of the decade's most prevalent styling touches.

Plymouth Valiant's large size and generous interior space—plus low prices—made it an exceptional value.

Pontiac's new Grand Am featured bold styling, powerful engines and European-style handling. Grand Am was available in both two- and four-door styles.

Pontiac's Ventura hatchback, like the Olds Omega, was a slightly restyled Chevy Nova. Like the others, the Pontiac version offered a hatchback coupe this year. The sporty Sprint package was still available, too.

Just what every young man wanted in 1973—a fire-breathing Pontiac Trans Am coupe.

Pontiac's big Catalina was popular with folks who liked a touch of sport in their big cars.

The Pontiac Gran Ville was a big, upscale family car.

Introducing the '74 Celica GT. Five-speed and all.

Pardon us, but we're going to use an over-used car term to describe the new Celica GT. "Loaded." Because it is.

Standard equipment on this fanciest of the Celica models includes: 5-speed gearbox, fat radials, styled steel wheels, tachometer, fully reclining front bucket seats with knitted vinyl trim, functional hood vents, racing stripes, rally clock and AM/FM radio.

Toyota's new Celica GT offers a lot. Without costing you an arm and a leg.

See how much car your money can buy.

TOYOTA

People were beginning to think about performance in a new way. Rather than emphasizing raw power, a new idea was to concentrate on good handling, decent output from a relatively small engine, and using a five-speed transmission to maximize efficiency. Toyota's Celica GT was a good example of that philosophy, and proved to be very popular.

Volkswagen announces a limited-edition Volkswagen.

Still one of America's most popular cars was the venerable Volkswagen Beetle. This year, VW even offered a sporty limited-edition version called The Sports Bug—and don't we wish we had one now. Despite its good looks though, the Sports Bug was just as under-powered as the regular Bug.

The Sports Bug

Bet you thought we'd never do it. Well, catch this:

Oversize radial tires. Mounted on snazzy mag-type wheels.

Indy-type steering wheel. Covered in simulated leather over thick padding.

True sports bucket seats. With contoured vinyl sides and no-slip fabric. To hold you comfortably while cornering.

Short-throw synchro stick shift. The faster you shift, the faster it shifts.

Spirited air-cooled engine. Cast with lightweight aluminum-magnesium alloy. Just like in Super Vee racing engines.

Four-wheel independent suspension. McPherson-design coil/shock combo up front. Double-jointed rear axle with independent trailing arms in back.

Special high-gloss paint job. In Saturn Yellow. Or Marathon Silver Metallic. Jet black trimming.

Options? All kinds. Like racing stripes. Flare-tip pipes. Stereo radio. And more.

If this sounds like what you've been waiting for from us, wait no more.

We built only a limited number of our special-edition Sports Bug.

After all, we can't make too much of a good thing.

Few things in life work as well as a Volkswagen.

As Volkswagen liked to remind folks, few things in life worked as well as a Volkswagen.

The 8:40 a.m. Grand Prix.

This is one automobile event just about everybody participates in.

The course runs several tortuous miles from home to work. It's an obstacle course. Filled with practically everybody else in town also scrambling to get to work by 9.

But just as Monaco has its Formula I car, there is also a specially built car for your 8:40 a.m. Grand Prix.

The Honda Civic.™

The Honda has everything you need to fight the freeways. Front wheel drive, rack-and-pinion steering, front disc brakes, four wheel independent suspension, and a peppy overhead cam engine that gets up to 30 miles to a gallon of regular.

April Road Test Magazine said it all: "Now...there is a new commuter car on the market; one which is large enough to be fairly comfortable, small enough to maneuver through rush hour traffic, gutsy enough to cruise at freeway speeds, and economical enough to operate all week on one tank of gas.

This amazing little vehicle is the Honda Civic."

"Clearly the automobile has

it all; it provides the most immediately viable solution to our traffic problems and does this with comfort, performance, economy, and low price. For center city commuters, Honda Civic is the car of the future. And it's here now."

Well, it's 5 p.m., and we're off and running again.

Gentlemen, start your engines.

The New Honda Civic
It will get you where you're going.

Upstart Honda launched a new car this year called the Civic—and it was a revolutionary small car. Similar in design to the original Austin Mini, the new Civic boasted very high quality and decent performance.

Fiat was still in the market, though it had a reputation for being somewhat delicate. Fiat countered that with this ad which included a testimonial from Europe's greatest stunt driver.

A TESTIMONIAL ABOUT A CAR, FROM A MAN WHOSE LIFE DEPENDS ON A CAR.

The flying car you see above is a Fiat 124.

The man flying the car is a Frenchman by the name of Rémy Julienne. Europe's greatest living stunt driver.

"In my work, if you want to stay alive, you leave nothing to chance.

"Obviously the car is everything. Before I drive a car I know it

100%. The body and suspension must be extraordinarily strong.

"And mechanically it must perform with great precision. It must do exactly what I want, exactly when I want it. Because if I am even one hundredth of a second off, it is goodbye."

Now, since in Europe there are 50 different kinds of cars to choose from, we thought you'd be

interested to know that in the more than 100 films Rémy Julienne has made he's done more stunts in Fiats than in any other car.

And the Fiat he prefers to drive above all is the Fiat 124.

A family car.

The biggest selling car in Europe.

Overseas delivery arranged through your dealer.

Chapter Five

1974

Running on Empty

Colorado's own Rebecca King was crowned Miss America for 1974, while, at the other end of the spectrum, President Richard M. Nixon was forced to resign the presidency on Aug 9, 1974. Vice President Gerald Ford, the man brought in to replace the disgraced previous V.P., Spiro Agnew, became our new president. It was a tumultuous year.

Godfather II won the Best Picture Oscar that year, but a much better film was Mel Brooks's hilarious *Blazing Saddles*—a spoof on Hollywood Westerns. Steve McQueen appeared in the blockbuster disaster film *Towering Inferno*. Big TV shows were "Kojak", "Sanford & Son", "The Waltons"—and the ever-popular "All in the Family."

Safety was a hot topic in the mid-1970s and the three-point seatbelt became standard equipment on cars—demonstrated here in an AMC Gremlin.

AMC ◤◢ MATADOR
NEWEST MID-SIZE FOR 1974

This is one mid-size car you've never seen before. The roomy AMC Matador coupe.

With sweeping, clean lines. Low profile. And plenty of window area for all-around vision. Test drive the new Matador. And see why experts are already calling it America's sportiest new car.

American Motors brought out its all-new mid-size Matador Coupe, which won immediate acclaim from the motor press.

AMC GREMLIN
RELIEVE THE FUEL SHORTAGE

AMC Gremlin is the only U.S. sub-compact with a standard six-cylinder engine. Yet for all its engine, the car is very easy on gas. Averages over 18 mpg, depending upon the way you drive. And Gremlin still out-accelerates, weighs more, has a wider track, wider front seat, and wider back seat than any other car in its class. If you want to know what else Gremlin relieves, price one.

American Motors Matador
a whole new driving experience
AMC

A gas crisis developed during the year, and AMC responded by more aggressively advertising its popular Gremlin X.

AMC's Matador Coupe even had a role in the new James Bond thriller The Man With the Golden Gun. Shown inset are two characters from that film.

Roger Moore and Britt Eckland in The Man With the Golden Gun.

Sadly, this was the last year for AMC's big Ambassador. For 1974 Ambassador received a new grill and numerous refinements.

Getting a lot of airtime on the radio—and also on the eight track—was Barbra Streisand's hauntingly lovely "The Way We Were." Also popular was Stevie Wonder's "Living for the City" and Paul McCartney's "Band on the Run." And the King—Elvis—recorded a powerful version of the old gospel standard, "How Great Thou Art." But somehow, the Record of the Year award went to Olivia Newton-John's excruciatingly drippy "I Honestly Love You."

The auto industry's 1974 model year opened up, as tradition dictated, in the fall of 1973. Signs of turmoil were easy to spot. Everyone was worried about the availability of gasoline. A gas shortage had developed in late summer of '73, spurred by a slowdown in oil production by Middle Eastern producers. Gas prices soared overnight. The days of gasoline selling for 30 cents per gallon were over—gas was now 60+ cents a gallon and climbing, and while that might

Buick's LeSabre was one big coupe—and a very popular family car.

Also popular this year was the TV show Kojak—who often drove a Buick on the show.

sound inexpensive in the context of today's prices, it represented an overnight doubling of the cost. Worse yet were the lines at gas stations, which stretched for blocks, leading to frustration, short tempers and—occasionally—violence.

Most Americans were unprepared for the gas crisis. After all, never before in our history had there been a peacetime shortage of fuel. The vast majority of cars on the market were big—heck, even our small cars were pretty large—and the predominant engine choice among Americans was the almighty V-8. True, the Pinto, Vega, and Gremlin were recent additions to the marketplace. But as good as their sales were, the bulk of the business still centered around the American full-sized car—the Le Sabre, Caprice, LTD, Fury and all those other glorious, big machines.

Although the public was caught off-guard, some car companies almost seemed to have anticipated the gas crisis.

Actually, they had simply been lucky. The biggest beneficiary of fortuitous coincidental timing was Ford Motor Company, which for 1974 introduced a new, much smaller Mustang that seemed to be just the thing for the changing times.

The new Mustang was substantially smaller than the old; with its 96-inch wheelbase, it was more than a foot shorter than the previous year's 'Stang. Overall length was 18.8 inches shorter, and weight was reduced by about 500 pounds. Based now on Pinto mechanicals rather than mid-sized Torino, the new Mustang came with a four-cylinder engine as standard equipment—an engine no Mustang had ever had before—a sturdy 2.3-liter overhead cam unit. To a public that had drifted away from ponycars when the darn things grew obese, the new Mustang seemed a breath of fresh air. The undeniable appeal of its newfound four-cylinder economy made it the choice of hundreds of thousands of buyers. Mustang's low price tag of $2,895 was icing on the cake. For buyers who wanted more

---

1974
Top News Items

- Richard Nixon becomes the first U.S. president to resign from office. The Watergate break-in that seemed insignificant to many just two years before leaves a trail leading all the way to the White House.

- A new office machine called a "word processor" starts appearing in office buildings. It looks a lot like a souped-up typewriter.

- Highway speeds are limited to 55 MPH because of ever-increasing oil prices.

- India detonates its first atomic bomb.

---

power, a German-built, 2.8-liter V-6 could be ordered. Significantly, a V-8 engine wasn't available at introduction time.

There were improvements to the rest of the Ford line. Most American cars still came with bias ply tires, but radial tires, considered sort of a luxury item, were now standard equipment on high-end Ford models, such as LTD and LTD Brougham. Ford's Torino line featured mechanical upgrades, and here too, the high line models now came shod with radial treads. The advantages of radials were numerous: they rode better, lasted longer, gave significantly improved handling, and best of all (times being what they were) radial tires improved gas mileage appreciably. Had it not been for their higher cost, they would have become the standard tire for all cars, but that was still several years away.

Six-cylinder engines were no longer offered in the Torino line, a decision that likely had been reached long before the gas shortage appeared. A 302 V-8 was now standard, and engine options ran

Cadillac said its Coupe DeVille "most exemplifies the newness of Cadillac for 1974."

It was easy for buyers to fall in love with the Cadillac Eldorado convertible for 1974. This was a large luxurious offering and a great travel car.

Another sharp-looking Cadillac was the Sedan DeVille, a plush and pretty four-door hardtop.

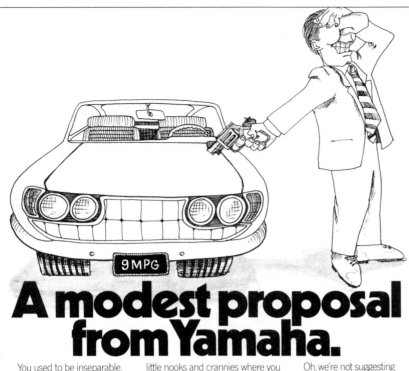

Response to the gas crisis was varied. Yamaha suggested buying one of their economical motorcycles (which, by the way, the author did). Sebring-Vanguard, based in Sebring, Florida, thought a better idea would be to bypass the gas problem entirely by buying one of their CitiCar electric vehicles.

1974

Top TV Shows

- All in the Family
- Sanford and Son
- Chico and the Man
- The Jeffersons
- M*A*S*H*
- Rhoda
- Good Times
- The Waltons
- Maude
- Hawaii Five-O

The Maverick line had few changes. The popular LDO (Luxury Decor Option) group continued as a very popular choice among buyers. The LDO included reclining bucket seats, steel-belted radial tires, and a host of appearance and trim items. Thunderbirds now came with the whopping 460 V-8 as standard, and also air conditioning. Pinto also got a larger standard engine, the 2.0-liter that had previously been optional. The little Pinto now came with front disc brakes as standard, and BR70x13 radial tires were a new option.

Over at the Lincoln-Mercury Division, the news was similar. The Monterey series now came with a 400-cube V-8 as standard, while the Marquis basic engine was the 460 V-8. Both engines came with solid-state ignition. Four-door models could now be ordered with optional mini-vent windows—and wouldn't it be nice if we could still get those today!

Mercury's hot-selling Montego now came with a 302 V-8 as standard, rather than the lumpy six of previous years. Montego also received new front and rear styling, an optional opera window for two door models, and an attractive "Embassy" vinyl roof option. The Montego GT was dropped.

Cougar was all new this year. It was, in effect, a revised Montego, whereas in previous years it had been based heavily on the Mustang. Mercury opted not to base the Cougar on the new Mustang II, since it already had a small sporty car in its imported Capri. Cougar came only as a hardtop—

up to a giant 460 V-8! And although Torino wagons came with Ford's unremarkable automatic transmission, all other Torinos still listed a three-speed manual transmission as standard equipment, in spite of the fact that almost no one actually purchased one, except for fleet cars.

Chrysler's New Yorker for 1974 was a competitor for Cadillac and Lincoln, was especially attractive as a four-door hardtop.

Three views of the handsome Chevy Camaro for 1974 show off its clean lines and sporty nature.

Thankfully, a convertible was still offered in the big Chevy line-up. This 1974 Caprice would be a great car to find today!

no convertibles were offered. Standard equipment was impressive for the time: 351 V-8, all-coil suspension, automatic transmission, power front disc brakes, power steering, radial tires—many of which were options on other cars.

The Lincoln cars were as big and plush as always. With their bold upright grilles and sharply drawn fenders, the Continentals simply oozed prestige.

Chrysler Corporation had a lot to crow about for 1974. The company was introducing all-new big cars in each of its divisions, and they were real beauties.

With all-new looks that did away with the unpopular "fuselage" look of earlier generations, the big Plymouth Gran Fury was as handsome a car as anyone could want. Broad-shouldered, upright and elegantly simple, this member of the "low-priced three" bore a resemblance to the Buick Le Saber—quite an accomplishment for a car that began at just $4,627. Standard equipment included V-8 engine (360-cid on the low-line Fury, 400-cid on Gran Fury), TorqueFlite automatic transmission, power steering and power disc brakes, plus an inside hood release.

The Plymouth Valiant and Scamp were upgraded to a 111-inch wheelbase—the same that the Dart had long been using. Duster coupes retained the shorter 108-inch wheelbase. The Plymouth compacts also got new energy-absorbing steering columns this year.

Barracudas had few exterior changes for 1974, but under the hood the 340 V-8 was replaced by a 4 bbl 360 V-8. The unloved (and unreliable) Plymouth Cricket was no longer in the lineup. Chrysler announced it would stop importing them

from England at the end of 1972, but a backlog of unsold Crickets kept them in dealers' showrooms through much of the 1973 model year.

At Dodge, the big story was the new Monaco series, which replaced both the old Monaco and the Polara. The Monaco, Monaco Brougham and Monaco Customs were entirely new. With formal, yet flowing, lines on a long 121.5-inch wheelbase, the big Dodges offered great looks and real luxury at very competitive prices.

Other Dodge models came in for minor freshening only. Newly available for Dart models were steel-belted radial tires. An electric rear window defroster, previously available only on Dart Sports, was now optional on all Darts. As before, the sturdy

1974
Sports Highlights

- Jimmy Connors and Chris Evert win men's and women's singles respectively at Wimbledon.

- Back again: The Oakland A's defeat the Los Angeles Dodgers in the World Series 4 games to 1.

- In Super Bowl IX, the Pittsburgh Steelers beat the Minnesota Vikings 16-6.

- West Germany (as it was called back then) takes the World Cup in soccer.

- Hank Aaron hits his 715th home run, breaking Babe Ruth's record.

Chevy buyers looking for top economy in 1974 would find it in a new Vega.

The Chevelle Laguna type S-3 was a sporty model in the mid-size Chevelle line.

A special Nova this year was the Spirit of America model.

Slant Six was the standard engine, while 318-cid and 360-cid V-8s were extra cost. Challengers and Chargers had minor improvements.

Dodge's mid-sized Coronet series got new styling, with the front end squared off a bit to give it a more modern appearance, one that shared a family resemblance with the new Monaco. The imported Colt, however, soldiered on with detail changes only. Better-built and more reliable than its Plymouth Cricket cousin, the outlook for the Colt's future was good.

The pride of the Chrysler line, of course, were the Chrysler and Imperial cars. Because these models shared basic body structures with the Dodge and Plymouth big cars, the Chryslers were all new this year. These were big machines, built on a 124-inch wheelbase and just shy of 80 inches wide. Newport anchored the bottom of the line, with

the handsome New Yorker next up the scale. The elegant Town and Country wagon, probably the most luxurious wagon on earth just then, was one

1974
Top Movies

- The Towering Inferno
- Blazing Saddles
- Godfather II
- Young Frankenstein
- Monty Python and the Holy Grail

The ever-popular Dodge Dart compact line included six models for 1974—two in the Sport series (top), two in the hardtop Swinger series (bottom), and Dart and Dart Custom.

The smallest Dodge this year was again the Colt, shown here in its popular hardtop version.

step up, and at the top of the mountain stood the all-new Imperial. This was without a doubt the best-looking Imperial in years, with modern, upright styling that bespoke taste and elegance. The front-end styling mimicked the popular Lincoln Mark IV, but its waterfall grille was more graceful. Imperials this year offered a four-wheel disc brake system—the first ever for an American family car.

It was a fairly quiet year over at market-leader General Motors. GM engineers were concentrating on development of new 5-mph safety bumpers, new seatbelts, new emission controls, plus preparing for its first attempt at offering some really far-out new technology—air bags. Folks were skeptical about the air bag concept, but GM had decided to give it a try.

Buick had introduced its new Apollo series—a re-badged Chevy Nova—in mid-1973, and that car returned with little new. Apollos offered the Chevy six as standard equipment, with a 350 V-8 also available. Century models got styling updates and more massive bumpers. The big story was in the full-size Buicks. Electra and Le Sabre were redesigned for 1974. With beautiful new styling that featured formal rooflines and a bold, rearward-flowing character line on the body sides, the new Buicks showed all that was great in American large cars. Riviera was also restyled this year. The gorgeous fastback styling of the previous generation hadn't caught on with buyers, so for 1974, Riviera got a new, squared-off roofline and a more sedate front-end treatment. It was a safe bet that the new Riviera wouldn't turn off many buyers—it was too conventional looking to offend anyone.

The Cadillac line received new roofs for the two-door Calais and Coupe de Ville, with a large, fixed rear quarter opera window. A padded vinyl half-top was a popular addition. Instrument panels and

front-end styling also were new. The Eldorado convertible and coupe returned with minor changes.

Chevrolet had plenty of news for 1974. Camaro received new styling up front, with a handsome egg crate grille, new turn signal lamps and new bumpers. The big Chevy line had new styling too, with more formal front-end styling, and new, formal roofs for two-doors. Caprices got new sound-deadening materials, making them substantially quieter than before. Malibu Classics also saw new grilles; a pseudo-Mercedes look that seemed a bit too formal for what was, after all, a family car for young couples. Opera windows, too, appeared on the mid-sized Chevy line. Corvettes came in for some changes in appearance. A new, soft rear bumper cover changed the look out back—the view other drivers saw most often. A new "Gymkhana" suspension system was optional.

Monte Carlo received a handsome new grille. With its long front fenders, opera windows, landau

1974
Music News

• The Ramones begin playing at CBGB a popular New York City club, starting what will become "punk rock."

• Riding on the nostalgia craze, and helped by the popularity of the TV show "Happy Days," Bill Haley's "Rock Around the Clock" is re-released and becomes a big hit.

• Paul McCartney releases "Band on the Run," which becomes extremely popular album.

Also popular were the Colt station wagon and sedan.

tops and bold, swooped styling, the Monte Carlo was extremely popular among hip, young singles.

The Nova line returned with minimal updates. Two-tone paint was a new option for the hatchback, and the Nova Super Sport model's striping was revised. With the 307 V-8 phased out, Nova buyers had but two engine choices—a standard 250-cube six or a 350 V-8.

At the bottom of the Chevy line, the Vega was gaining in popularity, in step with the increasingly tight supplies of gasoline. Vega's grille theme was new this year, a series of body-color cooling vents.

Like the other GM big cars, Oldsmobile's Delta Eighty-Eight coupes wore new roofs this year and they featured large, fixed rear quarter windows. Olds had one trick that other cars in its class didn't

have—a unique hinged grille that flipped backward if the car was involved in a minor front-end impact. Combined with the safety bumpers, the Oldsmobiles gave solid protection against high collision-repair bills. A new Regency Coupe joined the Ninety-Eight series. The Ninety-Eights also sported new stand-up hood ornaments, another of the style marks that would become ubiquitous during the decade. Cutlass and Omega series saw only minor changes. The Cutlass was one of the hottest products on the market, so only detail improvements, like radial tires, stronger bumpers and new three-point seatbelts with interlock, were added.

Pontiac also saw major changes in its big cars. The Grand Ville, Bonneville, and Catalina two-doors received the new GM roof styling, and the way Pontiac stylists interpreted it was especially good-looking. Pontiac's Firebird got new front-end styling this year. Engine offerings ran from a base six all the way up to a 455-cube V-8. Although the market for pony-cars was shrinking rapidly, the Firebird was one of the more popular offerings and the Wide Track division was determined to capture every sale they could. Also in the performance vein was the return of the legendary GTO nameplate, though this time it was stuck onto Pontiac's uninspired Ventura compact. Available on Ventura coupes and hatchbacks, the new GTO offered a 350-cid 4 bbl V-8 and manual shift (a three-speed came standard, but a four-speed was optionally available).

The smallest member of America's Big Four automakers, American Motors Corporation, was coming off a great year and aiming for another. AMC had big news this year, its first all-new intermediate car since 1967. Breaking away from industry traditions, AMC chose to introduce an all-new two door Matador coupe, while continuing to sell the four-door version with only slight styling revisions. The heart of the mid-size market was the two-door model, as witnessed by the unbelievable success of the Oldsmobile Cutlass Supreme, and AMC was banking on buyers to respond to a highly styled new offering.

That the Matador coupe was attractive is unquestionable. Its long hood, sloping fastback and colonnade hardtop-type doors, along with its unusual tunneled headlamps, marked this as an eye-catcher. *Car and Driver* magazine called it "1974's Best Styled Car." A sporty Matador X model was especially popular.

Returning to the AMC line-up with little change were the Javelin and Javelin-AMX, and the Hornet series. The big Ambassador also returned, offered only in four-door sedan and wagon models—no two-doors. The Ambassadors received new front-end styling—and these were perhaps the handsomest Ambassadors ever (as things worked out, they were also the last Ambassadors ever, as AMC discontinued them at the end of the model year). The popular Gremlin got new "free-standing" bumpers, which eliminated the beauty panel that normally hid the space between the body and the extended safety bumpers—a clever move by AMC. There were minor revisions to the sheet metal, and a new color-keyed grille was introduced. As was the case since 1972, a 304 V-8 was optionally available.

Also debuting from AMC was the new Jeep Cherokee sport utility. Based on the Wagoneer, the new Cherokee replaced the old Commando in the Jeep lineup. It was a larger, more comfortable SUV, exactly what the public had been asking for, and it quickly became a sell-out for AMC. Jeep once again had to increase production at its Toledo, Ohio plant, a happy event that was occurring with increasing regularity.

Ford took home *Motor Trend* magazine's Car of the Year award, for its timely and trendy new Mustang. The year ended with gas problems continuing to trouble America. Between the high prices and questionable availability, Americans were becoming more and more receptive to the idea of small cars. In fact, the July, 1974 issue of *Car and Driver* magazine carried a photo of something new on the market—the Sebring-Vanguard Citicar, a tiny, two-passenger electric car. It was capable of speeds of only about 30 mph and was hampered by a range of only about 35 miles, but it was a real car and it didn't need gasoline at all. Built by a small company formed in 1973, the Citicar sold surprisingly well.

However, the combination of gas crisis, high inflation and a stagnant economy caused a major drop in industry sales, with combined car and truck sales falling to 10,979,167 for the year, a drop of nearly three million units from the year before. It was a bad year for the car business, and the coming year would be worse.

The big Dodges were restyled for 1974, and were just about as handsome as a car could be. The look, which seemed vaguely reminiscent of a Buick, bespoke quality and class.

One of the 13 models in the full-size Dodge line was this good-looking station wagon.

For 1974, the Dodge Challenger came with a standard 318 V-8 and offered a new 360 V-8, plus a sporty Rallye package.

Ford's Pinto found renewed interest during the fuel shortage that developed this year. A larger 2300cc engine was available, plus improved suspension, a better sound-deadening package and redesigned brakes.

Ford Maverick was getting long-in-the-tooth by now, and probably would have been dropped from the lineup at the end of 1974 if the gas crisis hadn't spurred sales. New this year were optional front disc brakes and sturdier bumpers.

One of the hottest-selling cars this year was Ford's all-new Mustang. Substantially smaller, lighter and more fuel efficient, Mustang was offered as a two-door coupe, shown here, and as a hatchback coupe.

The Charger, Dodge's entry in the mid-size two-door market, could be ordered with a neat sunroof. Note the fender-top turn signal indicators.

Lincoln Mark IV was one of the largest coupes on the market and was a favorite of the wealthy. The Lincoln's out-standing styling feature was its bold, stand-up grille. Few people ever confused the massive grille with any other car.

Almost as expensive-looking as the Lincoln was the full-size Mercury Marquis Brougham, as this four-door pillared sedan shows.

Mercury's tremendously popular Montego MX Brougham showed new front and rear styling this year. An option called the Embassy vinyl roof was new, as were opera windows. The 302 V8 became the standard engine on all Montego models, and SelectShift automatic transmission was now standard on all station wagons. In the face of the fuel shortage, the newly optional 460-cid V8 must have seemed like overkill.

Anyone looking for a premium sporty car with an emphasis on luxury would have loved Mercury's Cougar XR-7.

Note the interesting body side sculpting on this 1974 Olds Cutlass Salon Colonnade Coupe. Cutlass continued to be one of the most popular cars in the country.

Cutlass Supreme didn't have the extreme body sculpting, but relied instead on quiet elegance.

Big coupes were still popular in America, and this Olds Delta 88 hardtop coupe was a good illustration of why. Another good example was the Toronado Coupe (inset).

Continuing its role as the anchor at the bottom of the Oldsmobile lineup was the Omega, shown here in its Hatch-back Coupe model. This littlest Olds was not a hot seller, but it gave Olds dealers an additional product to retail. A decent number were sold.

Perhaps you've forgotten but Plymouth offered a small range of trucks during the 1970s. Plymouth, trying to cash in on the public's enthusiasm for full-size vans and sport utility vehicles, sold a version of the Dodge van as the Plymouth Voyager—a name it would use again in the 1980s when it introduced its new minivan.

Trading on the well-known Duster nameplate, and aimed at the burgeoning Sport Utility market was this Plymouth Trail Duster. About the size of a Chevy Blazer, Trail Duster enjoyed reasonably good sales until the gas crisis eventually knocked it out of the market.

The big Plymouth was redesigned for 1974 and was more handsome than ever. The clean lines and tall glass areas made this one of the best looking full-size cars of the decade. This is the Fury Gran Sedan.

The bad and the beautiful—Plymouth's great-looking 1974 Roadrunner. The aggressive styling left no doubt that this was a hot street machine.

More in tune with the reality of the gas shortage was the Plymouth Valiant. The two-door Duster (top) came with Chrysler's old reliable Slant Six engine, but could be ordered with a 360 cid V8. Besides the coupe shown, the pretty Scamp two-door hardtop was also available. Family car buyers would probably have bought the Valiant four-door sedan, (bottom) which came on a longer 111-inch wheelbase this year.

New from Pontiac this year was a GTO option available on the compact Ventura and Ventura Custom coupes and hatchbacks. The GTO option included a three-speed manual transmission with floor shift, a 350-cid V8 with dual exhausts, special suspension, Rally II wheels, black grille, shaker hood and GTO identification front, side and rear.

Two views of Pontiac's Luxury Le Mans two-door for 1974.

A popular film this year was The Seven Ups—and also popular was this Grand Prix coupe (inset).

Buyers looking for a large performance car could find happiness with Pontiac's sharp-looking LeMans GT coupe.

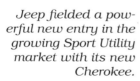

Jeep fielded a powerful new entry in the growing Sport Utility market with its new Cherokee.

Chapter Six

1975

The Tides of Change

The music industry had a pretty good year in 1975. Paul Simon's *Still Crazy After All These Years* was named Album of the Year. A popular new singing duo, The Captain and Tennille, burst onto the scene with their huge hit, "Love Will Keep Us Together," which went on to win Record of the Year honors. Nat King Cole's daughter Natalie made a big splash with her hip and bouncy "This Will Be," while song of the year was Stephen Sondheim's lilting "Send in the Clowns."

The scary hit movie, *Jaws*, and legendary producer Stanley Kubrick's *Barry Lyndon* were running in the theaters. George Burns and Walter Matthau gave good performances in *The Sunshine Boys*. Winner of the Best Picture Award, however, went to *One Flew Over The Cuckoo's Nest*, starring Jack Nicholson.

The fall TV season had many familiar shows— "All in the Family" was still number one, "Maude" and "Sanford & Son" also remained popular. Lindsay Wagner was "The Bionic Woman", and her show was surprisingly popular.

Shirley Cothran of Denton, Texas was crowned the newest Miss America.

It was a tough year for the economy, however. Fuel and energy costs had climbed out of sight, and a recession had taken hold of the country. Tens of thousands of American workers found themselves laid off. In spite of greatly reduced employment and widespread uncertainty for the future, inflation was

AMC came up with perhaps the most unique car of the decade when it announced its new Pacer. Available only as a two-door hatchback, Pacer was extremely wide by small car standards, giving it more interior roominess than other compacts and even greater than some mid-size cars. It enjoyed terrific sales during its first year on the market.

Individual reclining seats with an Indian print fabric were a popular choice among Pacer buyers.

The gasoline crisis spawned several unusual ideas, and the Buick Skyhawk could be considered one of them. The idea of a subcompact sporty car from one of America's premier big-car makers must have struck some old-timers as extremely unusual. Nevertheless, the Skyhawk was a beautiful, well-built machine.

Kojak was still hot on the trail of bad guys and high on the TV ratings list.

at the highest rate in years. This ran counter to all conventional logic, and out of the situation came a new term—*stagflation*, a time when a stagnant economy is accompanied by rampant inflation. It was a very worrisome period.

The car industry had, of course, settled on its new model range many months before the current economic crisis but nevertheless the car companies were able to field several new models that were just right for the times.

Chevrolet's big cars underwent revisions to their front styling, which made them look a bit more compact than the previous year—a move perhaps to make them appear less fuel-thirsty. Four-door sedans and hardtops got the new Colonnade-style roof that had already debuted on the two-doors. The ever-popular Monte Carlo received a new grille and taillights. Chevy Nova was restyled, with a squared-off, European-look roof for four-door models, thicker "B" pillars on two-doors, plus a more elegant grille and sheet metal. With high gas prices the norm, Nova was fast becoming a replace-

ment for full-size and mid-size cars among small families. In the Vega line, the long-delayed Cosworth performance model finally arrived. But with a price tag of just over $5,900, it represented, as one Chevy ad put it, "One Vega for the Price of Two." Sales results were a great deal less than inspiring.

Bigger news in Chevy small cars was the all-new Monza series, a subcompact aimed at buyers interested in economy, but who wanted something more substantial than a Vega. Although based on the Vega chassis, the Monza was about four inches longer, 180 pounds heavier, and was much more stylish. Available as a sporty two-door hatchback or a more formal looking two door "Town Coupe," the Monza line started at $3,570. For that price, a buyer got the 2.3-liter Vega engine, but for a bit more money a 262-cid V-8, the same used in the Nova, could be had. When installed in the lightweight Monza, the V-8 turned the econocar into a pocket rocket.

Buick got a version of the Monza, which the division called the Skyhawk. Available only as a two-door hatchback, only minor styling variations distinguished the Buick from the Chevy offering. Such a car coming from one of America's premier big carmakers was certainly an indication of the times—the first Buick-badged subcompact, debuting just a year and a half after the arrival of the compact Apollo.

Skyhawks were aimed upmarket from the Monza, however. They came with a richer level of trim, and were powered by the "new" Buick 231-cid V-6. This engine had taken a long and circuitous route on the way to resting under the hood of the Skyhawk. Originally appearing as a 225-cid V-6 in the early 1960s, low demand eventually led Buick to sell the tooling to Jeep. When

1975

Top News Items

- The last American troops leave Vietnam.

- The young Paul Allen and Bill Gates form Microsoft in Seattle.

- The Apollo-Soyuz orbital linkup shows a cooperative spirit in space.

- The Khmer Rouge begins a terrible revolution in Cambodia.

More traditional was the Buick Riviera. This was one of the most beloved big sport coupes on the market, while Mary Tyler Moore was one of the most beloved comedians on TV.

1975

Top TV Shows

- All in the Family
- Mary Tyler Moore
- Laverne & Shirley
- Maude
- The Bionic Woman
- Phyllis
- Sanford and Son
- Rhoda
- The Six Million Dollar Man
- The ABC Monday Night Movie

AMC bought Jeep, it decided to replace the engine with its own in-line six, and mothballed the V-6 tooling. Now, in the face of what looked to be a future of ever-increasing gas prices, Buick bought back the tooling from American Motors, did a bit of re-engineering to smooth out some of the engine's lumpiness, and decided to stake its future on V-6 power.

Like the Nova, Buick's Apollo received new "Euro" styling, including a very rich-looking grille. A new sub-series, the Skylark, was added. Apollo still came with a Chevy in-line six as the standard engine, but Skylarks came with the V-6 as standard.

The mid-size Buick line also got the new V-6. The Century and Regal series received new grilles. The appearance of six-cylinder engines in Buick's intermediate lines was proof that GM believed the gas situation would not improve soon.

The big Buick Le Sabre, Electra and Riviera models continued to offer standard V-8 power, with engines' sizes running up to the mighty 455. However, public interest in big engines was waning considerably.

Two famous names returned this year—Skylark and Special. Buick's entry in the compact segment, Apollo, was joined by a new Skylark coupe (top photo), while the Buick Century line now included a low-priced Special coupe (bottom photo).

Cadillac, of course, was a "big car" division, and the previous year had witnessed a dramatic drop in sales. Rectangular headlamps made their appearance on Cadillacs this year, and the big Eldorado received a major facelift. In April, the new Seville, a downsized Cadillac for the new era, debuted. However, since it was marketed as a 1976 model, we'll cover it in the next chapter.

Chrysler was another big car division that had suffered a serious decline in sales the previous year. To fight back, the company introduced a new mid-sized specialty model, the Chrysler Cordoba. Available only as a two-door hardtop, the Cordoba simply radiated class. Cleanly styled, with tunneled head-lamps and a hint of Monte Carlo in its profile, the Cordoba quickly became a "must-have" car for young

professionals. The rest of the Chrysler line was mostly carryover, including the top-of-the-line Imperial.

A new car company appeared this year, Bricklin, the maker of an exciting new sports car. Designed to compete with Chevy's beloved Corvette, the Bricklin was the brainchild of self-proclaimed maverick Malcolm Bricklin. Powered by an AMC 360-cid V-8, the Bricklin's main appeal was its sexy gull-wing doors, a bit of pizzazz that garnered an incredible amount of publicity.

At Dodge, the popular Dart line received that staple styling gimmick of the mid-1970s—a stand-up hood ornament. The Coronet line added a two-door model, its first in several years. Coronets came with the old Slant Six engine as standard equipment, but most buyers opted for the V-8, probably

The three good-looking Cadillacs on this page are the Eldorado Convertible and Coupe, and the Calais sedan.

Racing Legend Al Unser was the winner of the 1970 Indianapolis 500, driving the Johnny Lightning 500 Special at an average speed of 155.749 mph.

Buick's Wildcat for 1970 was a big car—sporty and sumptuous.

America's first subcompact car debuted in 1970 and it came from America's premier small car company, American Motors Corporation. The innovative Gremlin quickly became a top-seller for AMC.

The full-size Chevrolet Impala could be mild or wild—like this 454-cid V-8 convertible.

Buick Skylark for 1970 was an intermediate, or mid-size car, offering roominess and style.

Then, as now, the Corvette was still the ultimate thrill ride for many. This is a 1970 model.

The tough-looking 1970 Pontiac Firebird Trans Am had a purposeful style—one look and you knew it was a hot car.

A rare and wonderful machine was the 1970 Chrysler Hurst 300, a full-size performance car from a legendary maker.

Dodge's Charger R/T for 1970 was a powerful ponycar.

Ford's 1970 Torino sported clean lines—especially in the GT trim shown here.

America's original ponycar, the Ford Mustang, could be a docile economy car or a high-powered brute.

One of the sharpest cars of the decade debuted in 1970. Chevy's Monte Carlo was a mid-size luxury coupe that appealed to younger buyers.

In 1971, Gene Hackman gave one of the best performances in his long career when he played detective Popeye Doyle in *The French Connection*.

One of the most rarest special edition vehicles ever produced by Jeep was the 1971 Commando SC-1, which featured orange paint with black striping, fancy wheel covers and a V-6 engine.

The 1971 Dodge Challenger—Dodge's entry in the ponycar market—looks just as handsome today as it did then.

The last year for Plymouth's hot GTX was 1971 when it arrived with the rest of Plymouth's redesigned mid-size cars.

Certainly, anyone shopping for a small American car in 1971 couldn't be faulted for being attracted to the Chevy Vega. Unfortunately, poor design and multiple quality problems dogged the Vega right from the start.

Corvette always had a strong following, and this 1972 model shows why.

Toyota found itself with a hit when it entered the small, sporty car market with its pretty little Celica. Priced at $2,848, it was no wonder!

Toyota offered a wide range of models even in 1972, including the Corolla, Celica, Corona and Mark II shown here.

Lincoln had been the car of presidents for many years and the official White House limousine was this custom-built 1972 Lincoln.

IT TAKES SOMETHING PRETTY STRONG TO MAKE PEOPLE TRADE IN THEIR VOLKSWAGENS.

Leave it to gutsy American Motors to take a plain subcompact economy car, stuff a 304-cid V-8 into it, paint it wild colors (like the purple shown here) and top it off with racy striping. The result was the smallest and least expensive muscle car on the market—and the prettiest subcompact.

Buick Skylark GS Stage I was an unusual device—a muscle car for gentlemen! Despite its rich Buick trim, it was still a screaming machine when you opened it up.

Hot cars were the ones we talked about most in the early '70s and the Mustang Mach I was a favorite of many.

How many people remember that TV's Lou Grant drove an Austin Marina like this 1973 model?

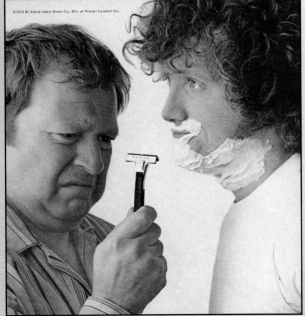

The generation gap was still talked about in 1973, and it was the theme of this humorous magazine ad. Schick razors are made in the author's hometown of Milford, CT.

Jeep offered this wild CJ-5 Super Jeep with racy stripes, fancy seats and trim for just one year—1973.

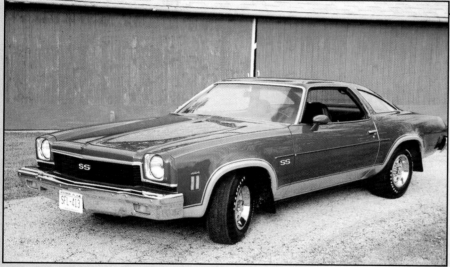

Chevrolet always had hot cars in the lineup, and one of them was this 1973 Chevelle Super Sport.

When Ford introduced its new, smaller Mustang in 1974, powered by a standard four-cylinder engine, it caught the public's imagination and quickly became a top seller for Ford. More elegant than racy, it mixed great styling with good fuel economy.

Mercury didn't get a version of the Mustang II, preferring instead to keep on importing the fine-looking Mercury Capri from Germany.

The big Lincoln Continental came in two- and four-door models for 1975.

James Bond showed the proper way to drive AMC's Hornet Hatchback in the film *The Man With the Golden Gun.*

One of America's top drivers, Mark Donahue, drove the Penske-prepared AMC Matador coupe for 1974.

In 1974 and 1975, America actually had a rival to the Corvette—Malcolm Bricklin's Bricklin safety sports car. Gull-wing doors made it a stand out, and with its V-8 power, it offered performance about equal to Corvette. This is a 1975 model.

AMC Gremlin for 1975 was one of America's favorite economy cars.

1976 Pontiac Firebird sports what wags referred to as a "screaming chicken" hood decal. This was a particularly attractive and popular car for Pontiac, and a real image-maker.

Chevy's Vega received updated styling throughout the years of its production and always managed to stay fresh and attractive.

Here's a sharp-looking coupe for a young family. The 1976 Oldsmobile Cutlass S Colonnade coupe featured new front-end styling.

Out in Kalamazoo, Michigan, tiny Checker Motors was still building its famous taxicabs, as well as a line of Checker Marathon passenger cars. As the company noted in its 1976 sales brochure, "Being Practical is Never Out of Style."

How many readers out there still have white suits with black shirts hanging in the back of their closets? Regardless of how you feel about Disco, it was one of the cultural phenomena of the era.

After the company that built the tiny CitiCar electric vehicle went out of business, the product was redesigned by another firm and reintroduced on the market as the ComutaCar. These cars were the most successful electric vehicles of the decade.

FREE TEST DRIVE
For the name of the dealer in your area, send us your name, address and phone number in our postage-paid envelope. Mark the envelope "FREE TEST DRIVE".

comuta-car

Lincoln Mark V was another in the long line of successful Marks from Lincoln.

Ford scored another hit with its all-new Mustang for 1979.

Mustang also offered a Cobra model, which obviously fascinates this young lady.

The big Chrysler New Yorker Brougham featured a refined grille design and new luxury interiors, plus new exterior colors.

because it was fairly small, at 318 cubic inches, and thus not as bad a gas-guzzler as some. Dodge Charger had all-new styling. With tunneled headlamps, a more formal roofline and elegant touches throughout, it was obvious the Charger was now set to compete with the Monte Carlo and other entries in the mid-size specialty market. The Monaco line still used the same body as previously, but models were revised and featured new standard equipment.

Ford was perhaps the luckiest car company in 1975. A few years earlier it had decided to redesign its Maverick/Comet series, in the process making them larger, roomier, and more stylish. As the announcement day approached, however, Ford noted increased interest in fuel-efficient cars. The company decided to retain the current Maverick/Comet and move their replacements up market a bit, creating a new luxury compact class in the process.

The new cars were the Ford Granada and Mercury Monarch. Built on a 109.9-inch wheelbase, their size was what passed for compact back then, but which would soon be considered intermediate, as America began a long and arduous rethinking of car sizes. Granada came with a 250-cid six standard, but Ford's 302 V-8 was a popular option, especially among folks moving down from a full-sized car. Priced at around $3,700 base, Granadas typically went out the door with a much higher price tag, since buyers usually opted for the automatic transmission, power steering and brakes, and of course, a radio. Air condi-

tioning, too, was a popular option. Ford's Maverick returned with little change. Listing about $700 less than Granada, Maverick's main appeal was price.

The full-sized Fords featured new grilles this year, and the hardtop model was replaced by a coupe with a large opera-style window—another popular '70s styling gimmick. In the mid-size line, a new hardtop coupe, the Elite, debuted as sort of a "poor man's Thunderbird." It was priced at a very reasonable $4,721. Thunderbird, by the way, introduced a new Sure-Trac anti-skid system for rear brakes. Pinto was little changed, though it did add a V-6 engine to the option list. The hot-selling Mustang II added a moon roof and 5.0-liter V-8 engine to its option list.

1975
Sports Highlights

- Arthur Ashe and Billy Jean King win the men's and women's singles at Wimbledon.

- In Super Bowl X, the Pittsburgh Steelers defeat the Dallas Cowboys 21-17.

- In this year's World Series, the Cincinnati Reds beat the Boston Red Sox 4 games to 3.

Motor Trend magazine's Car of the Year for 1975 was Chevrolet's new Monza, a sporty 2+2 hatchback.

Camaro offered a new Rally Sport model and featured a new wraparound rear window.

NEW CAMARO RALLY SPORT.

"Unfair," cried the ordinary cars.

"All's fair in love and cars," retorted Chevrolet, trotting out a knockout new version of Camaro, which was already one of the better looking numbers on the block.

The Camaro Rally Sport is a bright new option package available on either the Sport Coupe or Type LT, in your choice of five colors: red, white, silver, bright yellow or bright blue metallic.

The hood, roof, grille, rocker panels and rear end panels are painted flat black, with distinctive tri-color stripes and Rally Sport I.D.

Rally wheels and dual sport mirrors are included in the package.

Available options (shown) include front and rear spoilers and special 15-inch body-color wheels with white-lettered tires. (The special wheels are available only with the Gymkhana Sport Suspension.)

If you think it looks good here, wait until you see it in person.

Wait until you walk around it, sit in it, take it on the road.

But don't wait long. Production is limited, and we'd hate for you to miss out.

Now that makes sense

CHEVROLET MAKES SENSE FOR AMERICA.

Chevrolet

Chevy Corvette continued its reign as America's favorite sports car.

Hatchbacks were still the rage this year and Pontiac offered two—the subcompact Sunbird (bottom) and the compact Ventura (top).

Pontiac donated its one millionth Gran Prix, a 1975 LJ model with special red, white and blue trim, to the Detroit Bicentennial Commission in a ceremony on July 2nd that year. Seated in the car is Dr. George Gullen, chairman of the Detroit Bicentennial Commission. On the far right is E. M. (Pete) Estes, president of General Motors, and between them is Martin Caserio, Pontiac General Manager. Mr. Estes was general manager of Pontiac when the Gran Prix was introduced in 1962 as a specially equipped version of the Catalina Coupe.

Pontiac's Grand Am sported a rubber-like front snout that would flex in low-speed impact and bounce back to its original shape. As before, Grand Am was available as a two-door coupe in addition to this four-door sedan model.

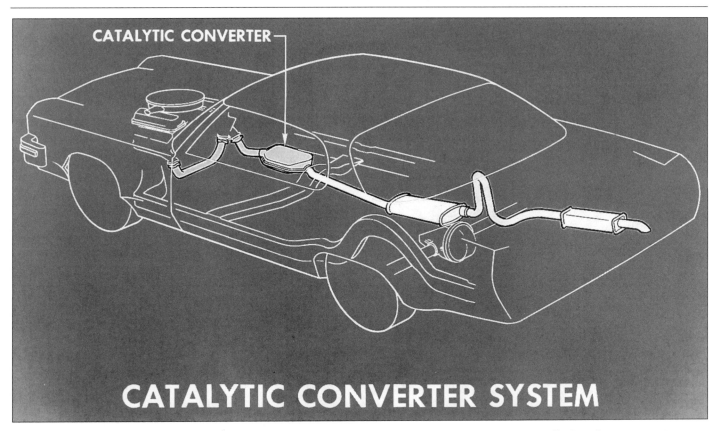

CATALYTIC CONVERTER

CATALYTIC CONVERTER SYSTEM

Fuel economy wasn't the only worry for Americans—cleaner air was a big concern as well. Catalytic converters came into wide use during the 1970s.

Pontiac's Astre series included this sharp GT Hatchback.

The Italian maker Fiat was still selling cars in America during 1975, and the tiny X1/9 won great praise in enthusiast magazines. It was an appealing concept—a low-priced, mid-engine Targa-roof sportster with styling by Nuccio Bertone. Priced under $5000, it was an exceptional bargain.

The venerable MGB was looking its age by now, but offered a lot of fun for the money.

Chapter Seven

1976

It's About Time

What a year for movies! Popular films included the political hit *All the President's Men*; the unusual and quirky *Network*; the truly frightening *Carrie*, starring Sissy Spacek; and the grimly fascinating *Taxi Driver*, starring Robert DeNiro. But the Oscar for Best Picture was awarded to *Rocky*, starring Sylvester Stallone, a movie so popular it spawned a string of sequels. Also appearing in that over-baked but unbelievably popular pugilistic epic was one of Hollywood's most enduring character actors, Burgess Meredith.

Music lovers also remember 1976 as a good year. After all, George Benson's recording of the haunting "Masquerade" was named Record of the Year, with Album of the Year going to Stevie Wonder's terrific *Songs in the Key of Life*. The song of the year, goodness knows why, was Barry Manilow's "I Write the Songs." Tawny Godin from Saratoga Springs, New York, was named the new Miss America.

Out there in TV Land, "All in the Family" was still among the most-watched shows, though by the fall season it had slipped down the charts. Cop shows were tremendously popular, and perhaps the best of them was "Police Story". Two nostalgic shows about the 1950s, "Laverne and Shirley" and "Happy Days", were big hits when the new season opened in the fall.

Car buyers were once again showing interest in large and mid-size cars, and sales of those began to climb out of the basement. The car market in general was getting better, helped no doubt by the many new entries that appeared. Most came in response to economic conditions of the previous two years, so they were aimed at the segments of the market below the traditional standard size car.

Beginning with the subcompact market, there was a hot new entry from America's favorite brand, Chevrolet. The Chevette came in recognition of the fact that the Vega was just an awful car and its reputation for poor quality was hurting sales. While very attractive to look at, the Vega didn't offer much in the way of interior space, especially in the rear seat, and its fuel economy wasn't up to the standards set by the European and Japanese imports. Chevette was simply a better, more modern small car than Vega. On TV and on the radio, Americans listened to the ever-present Chevette jingle, "*It's about time, it's about time, it's about time for a new kind of American car. It's about time for a new kind of car—and we've got it! Chevette is a new kind of American car!*"

Based on an Opel Kadett design, the Chevette was available in a single two-door style, but it

In an effort to counter price resistance among small car buyers, AMC fielded a really basic Gremlin so stripped of chrome that even the Gremlin figure on the sail panel was a decal.

AMC's Pacer Hatchback was a very unique-looking model in the compact field, and was highly praised by the auto press of the day.

Pacer added a slick four-speed transmission to the option list this year.

Chevrolet Division fielded a more competitive small car when it added the new Chevette to its lineup. Weighing less than 2000 pounds, and at least 17 inches shorter than any previous Chevy, the new Chevette really was "A New Kind of American Car."

1976 CADILLAC CALAIS SEDAN

Although Seville was the big news this year, the regular Cadillacs were solid values in the luxury class market.

offered several interesting trim variations, including Sport, Woody, and Rallye. Powered by an able 1.4-liter four, with a 1.6-liter engine option, Chev-

1976

Top Stories

- Steve Jobs and Steve Wozniak found Apple Computer in a garage after dropping out of college.

- Alex Haley writes "Roots," one of the decade's best-selling titles.

- Americans love their jeans; denim sales skyrocket, as "country" lifestyles become ever more popular.

- Jimmy Carter defeats Gerald Ford to become the next president.

- America celebrates its 200th birthday.

ette was rated at 28 mpg city and 40 mpg highway—really excellent numbers for the era. Its base price of $2,899 undercut the Vega's $2,984 base by only a little, but in the public's eye, the Chevette was clearly the wave of the future in small cars.

AMC's Gremlin returned with minor detail changes. It offered a choice of two six-cylinder engines, a 232-cid and a 258-cid, and the 304 V-8 was still optional too, though V-8 engines in small cars were not very popular by then.

Dodge was still offering its Colt, built by Mitsubishi of Japan, in the small end of the market. Not that there was anything wrong with that; the Colt was one of the better small cars available. It just seemed odd that GM, Ford and even little AMC had American-built small cars in their stables, while Dodge had to rely on an import—built by another company, no less.

Another new offering seemed to have a lot of potential—both good and bad. The new R-5 from French automaker Renault was a very modern design. It featured a responsive 1.4-liter engine, four-speed transmission, front wheel drive, disc brakes, and the soft, cushy ride that French cars were famous for. Capable of gas mileage of 30 to

Chevette was good-looking, in a fuel-efficient sort of way.

Chevy's Vega was still in the lineup, but poor interior room and a reputation for slipshod quality made it a tough sell. Chevy tried to counter the negative image by running ads that told of a 60,000 mile durability run Chevy made to prove the Vega engine's toughness. This year Chevy also included a five-year, 60,000-mile warranty on Vega's engine.

Chevy Nova continued to be a strong seller, at retail and even for police work. One Chevy ad showed a Nova police car with the tag line "Chevy Nova's a Wanted Car."

40+ mpg, it had the potential to grab a lot of sales. On the downside, French cars were known for being quirky, and Renault was still trying to live down its reputation for poor reliability and problems getting replacement parts.

Datsun's solid 610 series was winning praise for its rugged construction and splendid quality, though some magazines felt the styling was getting stale. The company's Honey Bee, however, was a favorite in the lowest price field. Ford's Pinto was another small car that seemed long in the tooth. Like the Vega, Pinto suffered from a lack of interior

room, mostly because at the time it was designed small cars were considered a second vehicle mainly for the wife or kids to toot around in. With gas prices at an all time high, small cars were now coming in use as a family's primary transportation, and roominess counted more than ever in the buyer's purchase decision. Mercury's Bobcat, introduced only the year before, was still selling well.

An interesting small car was the Subaru. Unlike other Japanese cars, the Subaru had front-wheel-drive, a feature seen only on some European cars, plus the Cadillac Eldorado and Olds Toronado.

The all-new Dodge Aspen series debuted, in four-door, two-door and station wagon models. The Aspen SE Coupe is show here.

The 1976 Dodge Aspen Special Edition Station Wagon was a perfect size for most American families, and offered a great combination of roominess, fuel economy and reasonable price.

Chrysler Corporation called the Dodge Dart "a car too good to replace"—a reference to its remaining in the model line, despite the introduction of the new Aspen.

Pinto (left) and Mercury Bobcat (right) were Ford Motor Company's two domestic small car entries. Ford Pinto had been the best selling small car in the critical California market since 1972.

Volkswagen was still the import leader, however, with its hot-selling Rabbit and Dasher front-wheel-drive models, plus its fading Beetle and Super Beetle.

Plymouth dealers finally got a new small car to sell, their first subcompact since the ill-fated Cricket. The Plymouth Arrow was built in Japan by Mitsubishi, same company that produced the Dodge Colt. Unlike the more family-oriented Colts, though, the Arrow was a very sporty-looking two-door hatchback.

Among the sporty two-door cars, the Chevy Monza was still an extremely popular offering. One minor quirk was that it offered a choice of a four-cylinder engine or a V-8, but not a six-cylinder engine. Buick Skyhawk and Olds Starfire, variants of the basic Monza body, each offered only a six—Buick's reliable and peppy V-6. New this year was the Sunbird from Pontiac—yet another variation of the Monza. The Sunbird came with a choice of a base four-cylinder engine or an optional V-6. Like the Monza, Sunbird came in both hatchback coupe and notchback formal two-door models. Pontiac still offered its Astre subcompact as well. As before, Ford's Mustang offered buyers a choice of four-cylinder, six-cylinder or V-8 engines, and the little ponycar's popularity continued. Over at Mercury, the Capri II, mid-1975 successor to the original Capri, was still well respected by enthusiasts, but the cost of building it in Europe was rising quickly, and it showed in the $4,235 base sticker price. It had been $2,395 in 1971, and was still only $2,688 in 1973. Sales were falling.

For many Americans, it made more sense to move up the price scale a bit to the compact segment. There, one could buy a lot more car for not a heck of a lot more money. American Motors had its Hornet line, two- and four-door sedans, a hatchback,

1976
Top Tv Shows

- Happy Days
- Laverne & Shirley
- The ABC Monday Night Movie
- M*A*S*H*
- Charlie's Angels
- The Big Event
- The Six Million Dollar Man
- The ABC Sunday Night Movie
- Baretta
- One Day at a Time

and the still-popular station wagon. AMC's Pacer was still winning acclaim from auto writers, so the company had at least one modern car in its stable. Yet, some dealers were reporting sales resistance to the Pacer, and inventories were climbing. Competing against the perky Pacer and the aging Hornet were a pair of all-new cars from AMC's toughest competitor in the compact market, Chrysler.

For 1976, Chrysler unveiled exciting new compacts for both Plymouth and Dodge. The Dodge Aspen and Plymouth Volare four-door sedans and station wagon models were big compacts, their 112.5-inch wheelbase nearly placing them in the

Ford gussied up the aging Pinto with the introduction of this Pinto Stallion model. The Stallion featured a blacked-out hood, lower back panel and a new textured grille. Black rocker panels and wheel lip areas, dual racing mirrors and a handling suspension were all part of the package.

Also available this year was the Squire option, which featured fake wood exterior trim, for the regular Pinto Runabout.

Another aging small car was Ford's Maverick, which could be dressed up by the addition of the Luxury Decor Option (LDO). Exterior highlights of the LDO included two-tone body paint, vinyl roof and full wheel covers, while interiors featured reclining seats, thick carpeting, and map lights.

Maverick two-door offered a new Stallion version, which included black grille and window moldings, black paint/ tape stripe treatment on the hood, lower body and lower back panel, plus large stallion emblems on the front fenders. All Mavericks came with front disc brakes this year.

intermediate category. Two-door coupes, on a shorter wheelbase, were also offered. Chrysler's timeless Slant Six was the standard engine, and V-8s were available. Like Ford's Granada/Monarch duo, the Aspen/Volare cars were so-called "luxury compacts," that is, small cars with the interior appointments and trim usually found only in big cars. Also like the Ford products, these new Chrysler cars were somewhat higher-priced than typical American compacts.

Taking yet another cue from FoMoCo, Chrysler kept the Dart and Valiant cars in production, although the original plan was that the new cars would supplant the old. There wasn't a big enough price difference between the new and the old, so most buyers chose the Aspen and Volare over the aging Dart and Valiant.

Fiat unveiled its new 131 series, which replaced the 124 sedans. Offered in two- or four-door models, plus a neat little station wagon, it was a typically clever Fiat design, marred only by concerns for Fiat's commitment to quality and service availability.

Ford's Granada/Monarch cars returned after a triumphant first year. Public admiration for the compact Fords was unusually high—the cars had really answered consumers' desire for a fancy car in a smaller size. There were good reasons for the popularity. After all, the Granada/Monarch had compact exterior dimensions, good interior space, decent fuel economy and handsome looks—overall a very nice package. Ford's Maverick and Comet were still around.

Mazda introduced its new Cosmo luxury coupe, with a powerful rotary engine under the hood. The Mazdas were known for being quick and technologically advanced, but their fuel economy was subpar, and finding mechanics skilled in servicing the odd rotary engine was of considerable concern.

Buick, Olds, Pontiac and Chevrolet all shared the same basic compact, which was marketed as the Chevy Nova, Buick Skylark (the Apollo name was dropped), Pontiac Ventura and Olds Omega. The cars had received new styling the year before, so for 1976, only mechanical improvements were seen. Interestingly, the Chevy, Pontiac and Olds all used the same in-line 250-cid six-cylinder engine, but Buick used its own 231-cid V-6.

Going up the scale one step further to the intermediate size usually offered greater interior roominess, better trim, a smoother, quieter car at not much higher price—but less fuel economy.

AMC's Matador series looked the same as the previous year, and sales were off considerably, despite a general increase in sales of larger cars. The big Matador sedans were solid, well-built cars but their dated styling was clearly not appealing to the public.

Chevy's Malibu Classic got new rectangular headlamps, stacked no less, and they gave the popular mid-size a much more expensive look. Dodge's Coronet, Ford's Torino and Plymouth's Fury had little new. The hot car in the mid-size segment was the Oldsmobile Cutlass, with its huge array of models, body styles, features and options. A new water-

1976
Sports Highlights

• The Cincinnati Reds keep at it, defeating the New York Yankees 4 games to 0 in the World Series.

• This time, it's the Oakland Raiders turn—they defeat the Vikings 32-14 in Super Bowl XI.

fall grille was featured, plus rectangular headlamps, and new roof treatments. Bodylines were tightened up and on the whole, the Cutlass was still the best looking, most admired intermediate car in America.

Big cars were coming back in vogue, but there was little new to excite people. The entire industry had been hard at work on smaller cars for the past few years and had left the big jobs alone. Now, buyers were back kicking tires, and increasingly, the tires were on big, V-8 American cars.

Chevy Caprice featured new rectangular headlamps, though the low-line Impala still had round ones. Chrysler's Newport underwent detail changes. Big Buicks also got new rectangular headlamps, and overall seemed larger and less elegant than before. Oldsmobile's Eight-Eight and Ninety-Eight series returned with new front styling and greater emphasis on fuel economy. But the big news in expensive cars was the newest Cadillac model, which actually had debuted in 1975 as an early 1976 model. However, the new Cadillac Seville wasn't even a big car. Based on an enlarged and heavily modified Chevy Nova chassis, the Seville was either a small intermediate or a large compact—take your pick. What it was, though, was a sensation.

Auto writers flocked to the new Seville, the first "international size" luxury car from an American company. Cadillac, realizing that many Americans still equated "small" with "cheap," shrewdly chose to

1976
Top Movies

• Rocky

• A Star Is Born

• King Kong

• Silver Streak

• All The President's Men

equip the new small Caddy with a higher level of standard equipment than its larger cars, and to price it higher than the others as well. Standard equipment on the Seville included power brakes, power steering, air conditioning with automatic temperature control, theft deterrent system, and a very plush interior. Powered by a fuel injected 350-cid V-8, the Seville appeared to all the world to be an American Mercedes-Benz. Its $12,479 priced tag was substantially higher than the Calais sedan's $8,825 tag, or even the Fleetwood Eldorado's $10,586. In all likelihood, the Seville actually cost less to build than the others, but Cadillac was trying to make an important point—small didn't necessarily mean cheap—and good

The 1976 Granada boasted improvements in ride and handling, interior quietness and better fuel economy. New options included speed control, power door locks, tilt steering wheel, AM radio with tape player and a Sports Sedan option, shown here.

Ford's Gran Torino two-door hardtop showed improvements to fuel economy this year, and now could be ordered with bucket seats, console, automatic parking brake release, and an electric trunk lid release.

things can come in small packages. They succeeded.

When funds ran out, Malcolm Bricklin's car venture ended in its second year of production. Down in Florida, the little Citicar ran into trouble when *Consumer Reports* magazine tested one of the little electrics, and rated it Not Acceptable.

The year ended on a high note. Industry car sales were 9,960,590—up about a million and a half from the year before. Chrysler Corporation's Dodge Aspen and Plymouth Volare won *Motor Trend*'s Car of the Year award, and 1977 looked to be an interesting year.

1976
Music News

- That wild hard-rock group, Kiss, makes their television debut on ABC.

- The Who is the first rock band to use lasers in their shows.

- Bruce Springsteen is caught trying to sneak into Graceland to visit Elvis.

Big cars weren't as popular now as they had been in 1970, but they still were the first choice for hundreds of thousands of Americans. Among big cars, the Ford LTD Landau was a particularly appealing selection. New this year was the option of four-wheel disc brakes.

Mustang II offered a super sporty version for 1976—the Cobra II. It featured wide stripes running the length of the car, spoilers front and rear and non-functional hood scoops.

Ford's Cobra II marked a sort of renaissance for ponycars. Though they were smaller and less powerful, their fuel economy was at least acceptable and they were more in tune with the times.

It's kind of hard to tell the 1976 Mercury Cougar two-door from the 1976 Montego two-door, isn't it? The Cougar is the one on top.

Rounding out the Mercury line for 1976 was the Mercury Comet and the Mercury Montego MX Brougham sedan.

Oldsmobile's Starfire came in plain coupe or fancy GT coupe versions.

Oldsmobile had a full lineup this year. Besides the subcompact Starfire, Olds dealers offered the beautiful Cutlass Supreme (foreground), the Omega Brougham (right) and the handsome Delta 88 Royale. This particular Olds 88 is a Crown Landau coupe.

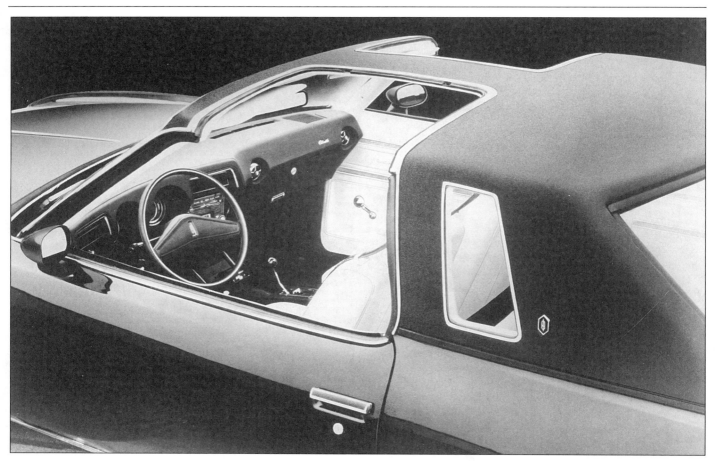

Two-door models in Olds' popular Cutlass series offered this sharp hatch roof, which featured two removable tinted glass panels.

A great size for an average American family, the Cutlass S Colonnade hardtop sedan was spacious, practical and very attractive. Note the "aerodynamic" grille.

The Plymouth Arrow rode a 92-inch wheelbase and was offered in three price classes—the Arrow 160 (background), the Arrow GS (right) and the top-line Arrow GT (left).

The Arrow could even be converted into a camper by the addition of this tent that fit over the open hatch.

Lindsay Wagner was a popular TV star with her hit show, The Bionic Woman.

Auto racing was growing in popularity. This amazing photo shows some of the biggest names in auto racing as they duel it out in an IROC race on September 18, 1976. The inset photo shows the winner—Buddy Baker.

Nissan still went by the brand name Datsun back then, and one of the most popular Datsuns was the low-price Datsun Honey Bee.

In the days before Click and Clack, the Tappet Brothers, there weren't any jokes about Peugeots. The cars were known as classy, well-designed machines, and their soft ride was legendary. Their lack of a far-ranging dealer body, and troubles finding replacement parts held down sales of Peugeots. Even so, TV's favorite thread-worn detective, Lt. Columbo, a huge fan of Peugeots, drove one on the program.

Jeep Corporation, then a division of American Motors Corporation, introduced the new CJ-7, which offered greatly increased interior roominess, better ride and handling, plus the availability of a good-looking fiberglass hardtop. An automatic transmission was offered for the first time on a Jeep CJ vehicle.

With its twin hood scoops, wide tires and bold graphics, Pontiac's awesome Firebird Formula was one hot car that couldn't be ignored.

Motor Trend magazine named the Dodge Aspen/Plymouth Volare twins 1976 Cars of the Year.

Chapter Eight

1977

America Learns A New Word

The best science fiction movie of all time—*Star Wars*—thrilled audiences this year with a fabulous combination of the most advanced special effects ever seen up to that point, and a timeless story of good conquering evil. Other classic movies debuting that year were *The Good-bye Girl*, starring Marsha Mason, and *Saturday Night Fever*, starring a disco-dancing John Travolta. Copping the Oscar for Best Picture, however, was Woody Allen's *Annie Hall*.

In music, we loved the Album of the Year, *Rumours*, by Fleetwood Mac. Tied for Song of the Year were "Love Theme from A Star is Born (Evergreen)," recorded by Barbra Streisand, and "You Light Up My Life," recorded by Debby Boone—who also won Best New Artist of the Year. The Bee Gees

were high on the charts with "How Deep is Your Love." Rock-n-Roll's King, Elvis Presley, died unexpectedly on August 16, 1977—and the loss was too great for words.

There was a startling sight at that year's Indianapolis 500 race. Car number 27 was piloted by Janet Guthrie, the first woman ever to drive at Indy. Ms. Guthrie didn't win the race, but she did shatter a glass ceiling, and that was even more important.

In Atlantic City, New Jersey, Dorothy Benham from Edina, Minnesota, was crowned the newest Miss America. Meanwhile, out on Long Island, Lilco, the Long Island Lighting Company, added two orange-and-white electric Citicars to its fleet of vehicles used by meter readers.

For 1977 AMC's Gremlin received handsome new styling, including new front fenders and grille, plus the sharp-looking new side stripe for the "X" package.

A new AMX appeared. Based on the Hornet hatchback, the full name of this model was the Hornet AMX, placing it in the Hornet series. A choice of a 258-cid six-cylinder engine or a 304 V-8 was offered.

The sleek Matador coupe was still involved in racing, even as sales of new Matadors sank.

In limited production this year was the new Jeep CJ-5 and CJ-7 Golden Eagle. Included were a large golden eagle hood decal and special body and grille striping, along with fender flares and gold styled-steel wheels. The exterior color was Oakleaf Brown, with a tan Levi's top. A roll bar and a rear-mounted spare were also included.

1977 Lightning Offenhauser Indianapolis 500 Race Car:
Driven by Janet Guthrie, the first woman to drive at Indy.

Shattering a glass ceiling this year was Janet Guthrie, the first woman to drive in the famed Indianapolis 500.

One of the most significant changes ever to occur in automotive product design took place in 1977. For the first time in memory, America's favorite full-size cars actually grew smaller than the previous year's. It was a change so dramatic that it ended up on the front pages of every buff magazine, as well as most of the top-ranked business journals of the day, and it spawned a new buzzword—*downsizing*. This change in product direction was in response to the fuel crisis America had experienced, it was clearly

the shape for cars of the future, and mighty General Motors was leading the way.

Chevrolet introduced all-new Caprice and Impala models, and they were markedly smaller than the 1976 models. Noticeably taller, more compact, upright and yet very handsome, the new full-sized Chevrolets were a revelation. Bodies were more than ten inches shorter in overall length, four inches narrower, and sat on a wheelbase that was 5.5 inches shorter—yet their upright styling offered approximately the same interior space as before. Weighing about 700 pounds less, the new Chevys had a lot of good engineering going for them. They handled better, cornered better, accelerated pretty well with their standard six-cylinder engine, and delivered much better real-world fuel economy. Even the optional 305- and 350-cid V-8s could go more miles on a gallon of fuel, thanks to the lower weight of the car. Plus, with prices that started just below $5,000 these new Chevrolets were a great value, too.

The rest of the Chevy line was carryover, beginning with the little Chevette, the aged and questionable Vega, the Nova, and the Camaro. The Z28 returned to the Camaro line mid-year, complete with a four-barrel 350-cid V-8. Chevy's Monte Carlo sported the stacked quad rectangular headlamps that debuted the prior year, but got a revised grille.

Pontiac made some interesting changes in its engine line-up for 1977. Its base six-cylinder engine was now the GM (né Buick) 231 V-6, rather than the old 250-cid in-line six that Chevy once sup-

1977

Top News Items

- As part of the "trucking" fad, CB radios gain in popularity, affecting regular TV and radio signals.

- "Roots" now a TV miniseries based on the top-selling book, attracts 80 million viewers—the highest-rated program ever.

- New York City gets a new mayor—Ed Koch.

plied, and the 455-cid V-8 was dropped. Sunbird sported a new standard four-cylinder engine, a durable, cast-iron 2.5-liter job that became known as the "Iron Duke."

Since all the GM divisions shared the same big-car chassis, Pontiac also offered new full-sized cars.

Lilco, the Long Island Lighting Company on Long Island, New York, added two brightly colored CitiCars electric cars to its fleet of vehicles used by its meter readers. Produced in Sebring, Florida by Sebring-Vanguard, the tiny CitiCars were the most successful electrics of the modern era.

Chevrolet called its all-new Caprice a "full-size car closely tuned to changing consumer lifestyles and matched with the nation's goal of conserving fuel and natural resources." The new Caprice was offered in coupe, four-door and station wagon models. A 250-cid six-cylinder engine was standard on coupes and sedans. Other engines included a 305-cid V8 and a 350-cid V-8.

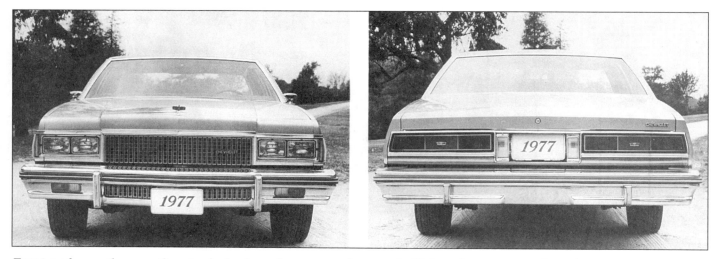

Front and rear, the new Caprice looked vastly more modern and efficient than previous big Chevys.

The new word this year was "downsizing." Newly introduced cars were smaller than prior models. Illustrating this were the new full-size Chevrolets. Despite reduced exterior size and bulk, the new Caprice and Impala models continued to offer generous interior space, especially in station wagon models. Two- and three-seat wagons were available.

The Chevy Monte Carlo continued to appeal to folks who liked high style in a mid-size two-door.

Chevrolet suggested buyers "Get a little road magic"—available in its Monza coupe and 2+2 hatchback.

Monza Coupe.

Monza 2+2 Hatchback.

Get a little road magic.

Racing great Benny Parsons occupies the No.1 position in this photo taken during the 1977 NASCAR season.

Buick Division also got new big cars this year. Shown is the all-new Buick Electra Limited four-door sedan.

The Catalina and Bonneville were variations of the basic body used on the new Caprice/Impala line and shared the many benefits that came with more compact exterior dimensions. Catalina came with the trusty 231 V-6 as standard, while Bonneville's base engine was a 350 V-8. Sunbird, Firebird and Ventura all now offered, either standard or optional, the V-6 engine. One interesting variation this year—Ventura could be ordered with the 2.5-liter, four-cylinder engine. Combined with a five-speed manual transmission, the four-cylinder Ventura yielded the highest gas mileage rating among American compact cars—an unusual accomplishment for GM's "performance" division—but these were unusual times. Firebird and LeMans both carried aggressive new styling up front, including rectangular headlamps.

There was similar news at Oldsmobile. New Delta Eighty-Eight and Ninety-Eight models debuted, using the new, smaller full-size chassis. The big Olds mod-

This Malibu Classic was one of the two models in the Chevelle lineup in 1977.

Trimmer in size and lighter in weight for improved fuel economy, the Delta 88 Royale coupe still offered traditional American big-car virtues of roominess, quietness and smooth ride.

Buick's Riviera coupe was new this year, based on GM's downsized big-car chassis. Opera windows and hood ornaments were all the rage this year.

els were still very impressive looking, despite their reduced bulk, and no one could ever consider them less than top-flight machines.

It was the same story at Buick. The division introduced its all-new, downsized Electra 225 and Le Sabre models. Le Sabre came with the V-6 as its standard engine, and with a choice of three V-8s—301-cid, 350-cid, and a 403-cid. Actually, the V-6 had shown up on the 1976 Le Sabre, but the few that were sold were notable only for being sluggish monsters. In the new downsized Buicks, the V-6 felt more at home. Electras came with the 350 V-8 as standard, and could be ordered with the 403-cid. The Riviera was also new this year, mainly because it shared its basic chassis with the big GM family cars. Sadly, the result of this cross-breeding was a Riviera that just wasn't as exciting or individual as it once was—Riviera this year seemed to be not much more than a Le Sabre coupe. The balance of the Buick line underwent cosmetic and detail improvements. As before, Buick's advertising theme this year was "Dedicated to the Free Spirit in just about Everyone."

Cadillac, GM's premier big car line, was celebrating its 75th birthday this year. Here, too, one could readily see the new downsizing that GM was pushing. The Coupe de Ville, Sedan de Ville, Fleetwood Brougham—even the vaunted Cadillac Limousine—were eight to twelve inches shorter in length, 3-1/2 inches narrower, and over 900 pounds lighter. These

1977
Top TV Shows

- Laverne & Shirley
- Happy Days
- Three's Company
- Charlie's Angels
- All in the Family
- 60 Minutes
- Little House on the Prairie
- M*A*S*H*
- Alice
- One Day at a Time

models now featured a 425-cid V-8 instead of the mammoth 500-cid. Seville was carried over with little change, since it was relatively new to the market and already a very "fuel efficient" design, but the Eldorado soldiered on in all its massive glory—and sold surprisingly well, too.

Chrysler's New Yorker Brougham still offered a body style that was fading away—the four-door hardtop. This beautiful car offered elegant interiors including optional leather upholstery.

Ford's Maverick returned for another season, pitched as before as a compact car priced much less than the more glamorous Ford Granada. New color exterior and interior appeared, along with new bodyside moldings.

Ford still offered its traditional big cars and bragged to the press that the company was "the Home of the Whoppers," a none-too-subtle dig at GM's downsized offerings. Ford claimed the LTD's traditional size and bulk provided more "road-hugging weight," a rather transparent effort to find new selling points for a car that was mostly unchanged from the year before. The Maverick was still in the line-up, though this was to be its final year—the hot-selling Granada was what buyers wanted in a compact car, not some outdated leftover from the 1960s. Pinto featured new front and rear styling, new bumpers, and some new colors.

Ford's big news at introduction time was an all-new, smaller Thunderbird. Based now on the 114-inch wheelbase intermediate chassis, the new Thunderbird was base-priced at just $5,063—a huge drop from the lofty $7,790 price tag on the 1976 model. Overall length on the new T-Bird was about ten inches less than before, and although the standard equipment list wasn't quite as inclusive as the previous model, the new Thunderbird was a

1977
Top Sports Highlights

- A.J. Foyt wins the Indianapolis 500 for the fourth time.

- Not letting history repeat itself, the New York Yankees beat the Los Angeles Dodgers 4 games to 2 in the World Series.

- Super Bowl XII sees the Dallas Cowboys victorious over the Denver Broncos, 27-10.

genuine bargain nevertheless, and sales took off.

Also debuting this year was a new LTD II to replace the old Torino and Elite models. The LTD II was, like its counterpart at Plymouth, a mid-size car badged with a name usually associated with a full-size car. Buyers could reassure themselves that they

Looking slightly Lincolnesque was the Dodge Royal Monaco, shown here in four-door sedan style. Offering full six-passenger seating and a smooth quiet ride, Royal Monaco came standard with a 400-cid V-8.

Ford's Pinto received new styling this year. The "soft" looking front end, sloping hood, horizontal bar grille and resilient headlamps housings gave Pinto a new lease on life. The optional all-glass rear hatch was new this year.

were, after all, buying an LTD model—even though it was less car than before. LTD II models included coupe, four-door, and station wagon styles.

Lincoln had a new model this year. The four-door Versailles was based on the Granada/Monarch chassis and was aimed to do battle with Cadillac's well-received Seville. Versailles came with a 351-cid V-8, and like the Seville, the standard equipment list was very comprehensive. Ford even copied Caddy's pricing strategy and tagged the Versailles at $11,500—about $1,900 higher than the

basic Lincoln Continental. Other Lincolns now came with smaller V-8 engines than before—a 400-cid mill, rather than the 460-cid. A new Lincoln, the Mark V, replaced the Mark IV. The new car was several hundred pounds lighter than before, and its bodylines were crisper.

Mercury also had "new" mid-size cars. The Montego, which had been such a hot seller just a few years earlier, was supplanted by an expanded line of Cougars. The Cougar line now included two- and four-door models, plus a station wagon, as well

A new Thunderbird arrived for 1977. Now competing in the mid-sized category, Thunderbird retained its classic looks in a smaller, more affordable package and sales were red-hot.

as the top-of-the-line Cougar XR-7 coupe. Like Ford's Granada, the Mercury Monarch now offered a four-speed overdrive transmission, allowing better over-the-road fuel economy to anyone who wanted a manual shift. This was the last year anyone could buy a Comet.

American Motors was in a fix this year. Sales of its Pacer had slowed considerably, its Hornet was looking almost ancient, its Matador coupe and sedan models were struggling against newer, more refined machines, and the market was turning away from small cars.

The little automaker did have some new products to show. Biggest news was the new Pacer station wagon. Although based on the 100-inch wheelbase, the Pacer wagon had a longer, squared off back end with obviously better carrying space.

1977
Top Movies

- Star Wars
- Close Encounters of the Third Kind
- Saturday Night Fever
- Smokey and the Bandit
- The Goodbye Girl

The car also looked less weird than the Pacer hatchback, and sales response was pretty good. AMC's Gremlin came in for some new styling, three years overdue, unfortunately, but better late than never. Gremlin's front end was shorter now, and the grille and hood design were dramatically improved. The "X" package got great-looking new stripes. Mid-year came a new four-cylinder engine, a 2.0-liter produced on an assembly line that AMC purchased from Audi. Gremlin offered three models this year, a stripped six-cylinder model and two Custom models—one a six-cylinder, one with the new 2.0-four. The V-8 engine was no longer available in Gremlin, a move enthusiasts bemoan today, though at the time it seemed the right thing to do.

The Hornet sedan, wagon and hatchback line was mostly carryover. A new Hornet model, however, was the Hornet AMX, which was a Hornet Hatchback with a sport appearance package and a standard 258-cid six-cylinder or an optional 304 V-8. Actual performance wasn't much better than a regular Hornet, but the Hornet AMX's styling recalled the best of the original ponycars, and most enthusiasts' magazines welcomed the new offering.

Chrysler Corporation had several new models debuting this year. From its flagship Chrysler Division came a new smaller car, the Chrysler LeBaron, available as either a coupe or sedan. Based on the Volare/Diplomat sedan chassis, even using the same wheelbase, this new Chrysler was not aimed at the high-end Versailles and Seville, but was supposed to carve out a healthy slice of market share by offering a fuel-efficient, modern-looking mid-size Chrysler at a price that would guarantee good sales volume. Indeed, the basic LeBaron sedan was tagged at $5,224 and seemed worth every penny of it.

Cordoba reigned as one of the most coveted luxury coupes on the market, and the big Chryslers—the Newport and New Yorker—continued to offer all the pleasure and comforts of traditional American luxury barges.

Dodge got a version of the new LeBaron, with a plainer grille and trim, and it was called the Diplomat. Designated a premium specialty intermediate, it was offered in coupe and sedan styles. Dodge decided to discontinue the Coronet nameplate this year, and replaced it with a line of intermediate size cars that bore the name Monaco. The big Monaco of the prior year returned as the Royal Monaco. Both the downsized Monaco and the Royal Monaco were offered in two-door, four-door and station wagon models. The small series could be had with either a six- or eight-cylinder engine, while the Royal Monaco came only with an eight. The Dart line was no longer offered, replaced entirely by the better-selling and more contemporary Aspen. Dodge's Charger was still available, and offered a unique Charger Daytona appearance package with wild two-toning and striping.

At Plymouth, the story was similar. The Valiant series, once the division's very lifeblood, was gone, as Volare continued to expand its appeal to buyers. The midsize Fury was facelifted this year, gaining quad rectangular headlamps in the bargain. In the full-size Gran Fury series, the Custom models were deleted, but a base two-door was

added. The cover of the July issue of Car and Driver magazine featured a wild looking new car—John DeLorean's gull-wing DMC-12. It wasn't available for purchase just yet, but plans were being made to get it into production.

It came as no surprise when *Motor Trend* magazine named the all-new Chevrolet Caprice its Car of the Year for 1977. After all, it was a tremendously significant new car, it was the size America needed, and Chevy deserved the prize, even though it was receiving it now for the fourth time in seven years.

The auto industry could count 1977 as one of its better years. A recovering economy, availability of fuel, and many new products combined to push car sales up over 11 million for the year. As the decade was nearing its end, things at last appeared to be heading in the right direction.

Also new from Ford this year was the LTD II, a mid-size car Ford hoped would attract buyers moving down from full-size cars.

Growing more handsome every year was the big Ford—including the LTD Landau sedan shown here.

Lincoln Continental Mark V was the latest generation in a dynasty of luxury cars to bear the Continental Mark designation. The traditional Mark grille and fake "spare tire" deck lid were retained, and new styling touches, like the functional front fender louvers, were added. Although about the same size as the previous Mark IV, the Mark V was about 400 pounds lighter for improved fuel economy. A Cartier day/date clock was included.

Mercury's Grand Marquis was a great example of a traditional big car in the American idiom. Cars like these once ruled the automobile market, now are becoming forgotten.

Mercury's biggest sales success was its Cougar, a car widely admired for its good looks and luxury features. The XR-7 coupe was Mercury's glamour car in the intermediate class. The hood ornament, landau vinyl roof and sculptured deck lid were styling touches that Americans craved.

The success of the Cougar line inspired Mercury to expand the lineup to include four-door sedans, station wagons and coupes. The XR7 coupe remained the style leader. Cougar ads often included a beautiful woman walking a cougar on a leash.

Up the ladder from the Delta 88 in price and appointments was the completely redesigned Oldsmobile 98 Regency, which came in four-door and coupe models.

But the new Pacer wagon was getting the most attention—and no wonder!

The Olds Toronado continued to be produced on a front-wheel drive chassis.

Pontiac's Firebird Formula featured new rectangular headlamps this year. The 'Bird was as good-looking a sporty coupe as anyone could want, and was a favorite among swinging singles.

Pontiac's Ventura was mostly unchanged this year but offered a 2.5-liter four-cylinder engine and five-speed manual transmission for top fuel economy. Despite the potential for maximum fuel savings, however, the six- and eight-cylinder offerings proved more popular.

Grand LeMans coupe from Pontiac was an intermediate, or mid-size, model. With the downsizing of GM's full-size cars, the mid-size models were now close to them in external dimensions. Popular on TV that season was the program *The Hardy Boys Mysteries*, starring Parker Stevenson and Shawn Cassidy.

Pontiac's LeMans GT was a member of a vanishing breed—intermediate size performance models.

Chapter Nine

1978

Things Would Never Be The Same

In 1978, Americans were examining their feelings about the country's wrenching and painful involvement in the late conflict in Vietnam. The topic appeared repeatedly in films that year. Two popular movies were *Coming Home* and *The Deer Hunter*, the latter of which won the Academy Award for Best Picture. On a lighter note, Gary Busey turned in a fine performance as the title character in *The Buddy Holly Story*.

Pop singer Billy Joel shot to the top of the charts with his hit "Just the Way You Are," which won the award for Record Of The Year, as well as Song of the Year. Disco was still the rage, and the Bee Gees won Album of the Year for their *Saturday Night Fever*, while Barry Manilow won Best Pop Vocal Performance for his hit "Copacabana."

On the tube, "All In The Family", "Three's Company", "Happy Days", and "Mork and Mindy" were all extremely popular. The beautiful young lady chosen this year to wear the Miss America crown was Susan Perkins of Columbus, Ohio.

In the previous two years, America's revived interest in electric cars slackened and by now had shrunk to nearly zero. After all, the economy was good, gasoline was abundant, if still fairly pricey, and the new cars being introduced showed exceptional fuel economy improvements. Production of the little Citicar had stopped.

There was a flood of new automobiles being introduced. The Big Three and American Motors all had exciting new products debuting this year. General Motors was continuing its downsizing program. Starting last year with the standard size cars, this year it was the mid-size, (or intermediate) automobiles that would see their bulk reduced.

This was potentially dangerous ground for GM to tread, for although most Americans knew in their hearts that the their big cars had grown too darn big,

In addition to two- and four-door models, Concord also offered a four-door station wagon and this sharp Concord hatchback.

Scrappy little American Motors was still in there swinging, launching its newest compact car. The Concord was heavily based on the prior Hornet series but featured important improvements in ride, handling, interior comfort and quietness. Concord styling was a hit with many Americans.

Hornet AMX was replaced by this restyled and refined AMX based on the new Concord Hatchback.

the average buyer of a mid-size automobile felt his vehicle was already just about the right size. Getting a customer to adjust his (or her) thinking would take some doing. But it was absolutely necessary. America's stated goal of improving auto fuel economy had allowed Congress to set Corporate Average Fuel Economy (CAFE) targets into law, and heavy fines were a threat to any automaker that failed to meet them.

Actually, most of GM's new mid-sized cars were quite attractive. Shorter in length than their predecessors by about twelve inches, some 600 pounds (or more) lighter, and narrower too, the new rear-wheel-drive GM intermediates still managed to offer generous interior space, though comparisons inevitably noted reduced hip room.

Chevrolet's new Malibu series replaced the former Chevelle/Malibu line. Offered as a two-door coupe, four-door sedan or a station wagon, the Malibu appeared to be no larger than the Nova—and in fact, its wheelbase was actually shorter by three inches! But inside—well, that was a different story. There, efficient design provided much more room and comfort than Nova could ever hope to offer. Plus, the standard engine was a smallish 3.3-liter V-6, so fuel economy was markedly better. Debuting along with the new Malibu was an all-new El Camino pickup that was obviously based on the new downsized Malibu body.

From its introduction, the Monte Carlo had been based on the Chevelle/Malibu chassis, and for that reason a new Monte Carlo was also debuting this year. The Chevrolet stylists really outdid themselves on this one, creating a style that looked both flashy and efficient at the same time.

Chevette continued to serve as the entry point for Chevy cars. A four-door model was added, something the market was looking for just then, and the line saw some minor additions to the list of standard features. The base Chevette Scooter two-door was priced at just $2,999.

The Vega was not in the line-up this year—at least not in name. However, the Monza line was expanded to include a new two-door station wagon, and it was rather apparent that this was merely the old Vega wagon with a new front end. Luckily for all, though, the dreaded Vega engine (which had become a veritable symbol of poor quality) was discontinued, so Monza now came with GM's rugged cast-iron four as standard.

A new Custom model was added to the Nova lineup, which by the way still included an optional 350-cid V-8 in place of the 250-cid six or 305 V-8.

1978
Top News Stories

- Louise Brown, the world's first test-tube baby, is born in London.

- Volkswagen announces it will cease production of the Beetle.

- Although it's been a few years since Nixon's visit, the United States formally recognizes the People's Republic of China.

Buick's new intermediate line for 1978 included the Regal sport coupe. A foot shorter and some 560 pounds lighter than the previous year, Regal could be had with a potent turbocharged V6 engine.

Side profile shot of the new Buick Regal shows its classic looks and square-cut roofline.

Camaro got a new look this year, with a body-color, soft nose section. Chevy's uninspired 250-cid six was standard, but 305- and 350-cid V-8s were available instead. Impala and Caprice were mostly carryovers, though they did benefit from some equipment changes.

Buick's Skyhawk returned with minor changes. The Skylark also looked relatively unchanged, but a Custom model was introduced. Buick's big announcement this year was its all-new Century and Regal lines, which were based on the new GM downsized intermediate chassis.

Century was offered in four-door sedan and station wagon versions, as well as a two-door coupe. The coupe and sedan models had an unusual fastback rear that made them appear to have a hatchback, but in fact both came with a conventional trunk. Regal was available as a two-door coupe in three trim levels: Regal, Regal Sport, and Regal Limited. The engine choices for the new mid-size Buicks were numerous—V-6s in both 3.2- or 3.8-liter sizes, and V-8s in either 305- or 350-cubic-inch sizes. Regal could also be had with a turbocharged 3.8 V-6 with up to 165 horsepower—a performance car for a new era.

The Le Sabre, Electra and Riviera lines were mostly carryover, though the Le Sabre Sport Coupe could now be had with the Turbo V-6 engine.

1978
Top Tv Shows

- Laverne & Shirley
- Three's Company
- Mork & Mindy
- Happy Days
- What's Happening!
- Alice
- M*A*S*H*
- One Day at a Time
- Taxi

Buick's advertising theme this year was "A Little Science. A Little Magic."

Pontiac's new intermediates were the LeMans and the Grand Am—the latter a nameplate that hadn't been used since 1975—plus the Grand Prix coupe. LeMans was available in two- or four-door

Another model in the new Buick intermediate line was the Century. Among Century two-doors, the flashiest was the Century Sport Coupe, distinguished by special paint and striping. The Century's fastback design made it appear to be a hatchback but in fact it had a conventional trunk.

A better view of Century's controversial fastback styling is shown in this photo of the Century Limited four-door sedan.

There was nothing controversial about the styling of Cadillac's Seville. Still a hit with luxury car buyers, Cadillac claimed that one-third of Seville buyers were attracted away from luxury imports.

Chrysler's Le Baron didn't sell in the lofty stratum of Seville and Versailles, but sold very well as a mid-sized alternative to conventional luxury-cars.

styles, plus a station wagon, while the sportier Grand Am came only in two- or four-door models. All rode GM's new 108-inch chassis. Grand Prix shared its body with the new Monte Carlo, but had a different styling theme. Pontiac was trying to imitate the bold styling cues of classic-era Duesenburgs, and those cues showed up most clearly on the Grand Prix.

The Ventura was gone, but its replacement, the Phoenix, was identical in most specifications and its styling was very similar. Why Pontiac chose to re-badge its Nova clone this late in the game is a mystery. Also gone from the lineup was Pontiac's Vega clone, the Astre, although like its Chevy cousin, the Astre wagon was renamed the Sunbird wagon. The rest of the Sunbirds were little changed from before.

Oldsmobile had a surprising number of new or revised products this year. Its Cutlass line was now on GM's all-new 108-inch wheelbase. Cutlass models included Aero-style two- and four-door sedans quite similar to the Buick offerings, plus a broad line of Cutlass Supreme coupes. Engine choices included the ubiquitous 231 V-6, an exclusive 260-cid V-8, plus a 305-cid V-8, and even a 350-cid for some models.

Starfires were now available with GM's cast-iron 2.5-liter four as the standard engine, and still offered the V-6 as an option. In the Omega line, the base F85 model was dropped, as was the Brougham Hatchback.

Oldsmobile also had important news in its big car lines. A new, lightweight V-8 Diesel engine was announced. Based on the 350-cid block, the Olds

Chevy Monza offered two hatchback models this year—an up-level one with quad rectangular headlamps and a low-priced "S" with conventional round headlamps.

Chevrolet added a four-door model to the Chevette and it proved extremely popular.

diesel was an attempt to combine big engine power with traditional diesel economy, and the results seemed nothing short of remarkable. A full-size Delta Eighty-Eight sedan, one of America's best known and best loved big cars, could deliver 30 mpg at average highway speeds. Long-term reliability of diesels was well known, so buyers felt they could rely on that in the new Oldsmobile engine. However, soon enough owners would find out that a diesel engine based on a gas engine design was not necessarily as trouble-free as a heavy-duty truck engine. Early in production, the Olds diesels suffered from soft camshafts that created production shortages while engineers tried to solve the problem. Over the long term, there was no end of troubles for the new diesel, and Oldsmobile's reputation took a serious hit because of it.

Cadillac's changes for 1978 were limited to detail improvements, new grilles and trim.

American Motors, struggling since the downturn in 1976, fought back as best as it could this year. Lacking the substantial funds needed to come out with an all-new car like the new GM products, AMC chose to perform a modest facelift of its dated Hornet, load it up with fancy trim and move it slightly upmarket. Renamed the Concord, and reclassified as a luxury compact, it was aimed to do battle with the up-level compacts from Ford, GM, and Chrysler.

Concord's designers did a first-class job with the tiny budget they were allowed. The shorter front end was quite attractive, while the die-cast grille and handsome hood ornament bespoke luxury in the idiom of the day. Ride quality was vastly improved, and additional sound deadening made Concord exceptionally quiet. Inside were available

some of the smartest interior appointments ever included in an American compact car, far and away the plushest seats and door trim of any car in its price range. Two-door Concords started at $3,749. The popular D/L luxury package, which included a vinyl roof, opera windows, digital clock, plush seats and much more, added just $200 to the price—an incredible value. Concord offered the same body styles as the former Hornet—two- and four-door sedans, a four-door station wagon and a two-door hatchback.

The Hornet AMX was gone, replaced by a very similar AMX based on the new Concord. Better-looking this year due to the revised front-end styling, the AMX sold in limited numbers.

1978
Sports Highlights

- Muhammad Ali might be "The Greatest," but he doesn't stop Leon Spinks from taking the World Heavyweight Championship in Las Vegas.

- Al Unser wins his fifth Indianapolis 500.

- This time, history repeats itself in New York's favor—the Yankees defeat the Dodgers, 4 games to 2, just like last year.

- Super Bowl XIII turns out to be the lucky one for the Steelers, who defeat the Cowboys 35-31.

- Argentina defeats the Netherlands in soccer for the World Cup.

Chevy's biggest news this year was its all-new Malibu mid-size cars. A foot shorter and 540-968 pounds lighter than last year's cars, the new Malibu was more modern in every way. A 3.3-liter V-6 engine was standard except in California, where a 3.8-liter V-6 was the standard engine.

Chevrolet Impala sport coupe was enjoying great popularity again this year.

During this year when so many new products were introduced one of the most important was the new Dodge Omni. Called a four-door compact by its manufacturer, it sold mainly against subcompact offerings like AMC Gremlin and Chevy Chevette. Its modern front-wheel-drive design offered room and comfort that were superior to its domestic competitors.

Dodge's Diplomat station wagon offered luxury and comfort that rivaled traditional full-size wagons, with fuel economy competing with compacts, and was a favorite among young families.

Gremlin was in its final year. For 1978, the stripes for the X package were again revised, this time running in a thick band along the bottom of the car. A new Gremlin GT appeared, a wild-looking thing with bold, fat side stripes, big wheels and tires, wheel flares and a front air dam. The fading Matador line saw scant changes.

Chrysler had big news in transmission design this year. A new lock-up torque converter debuted on the TorqueFlite automatic transmission, providing improved fuel economy. Also new was a 40-channel CB radio—a recent fad had created strong demand for CBs.

A Town & Country wagon joined the LeBaron line this year. The Slant Six was now the standard engine, though the 318- and 360-cid V-8s were also available. A new, budget "S" series was added.

Cordoba received new front-end styling, with

Ford brought the most successful new car ever introduced in Europe, its Fiesta, to America. Its goal was to attract buyers interested in the engineering features and maximum fuel economy that were a hallmark of European small cars. Featuring front-wheel drive, it was powered by a 1.6-liter four-cylinder engine with four-speed transmission. Four trim levels were offered—standard, Decor, Sport (shown) and Ghia.

Ford liked to think of itself as America's small car headquarters. Besides the new Fiesta, Ford dealers also had the Pinto and Mustang II to offer—a solid line of economical cars.

vertically stacked rectangular headlamps, while the rest of the Chrysler line was limited to small changes and improvements.

Dodge had a major new product for 1978. The division at last fielded an American-built sub-compact car. The old saying, "last out, best dressed," certainly applied to the new, small Dodge. The Omni was a four-door hatchback sedan that closely resembled the highly respected VW Rabbit. Built on a generous 99-inch wheel-base, Omni offered plenty of room for four adults. It was the first front-wheel-drive compact from an American company. Powered by a VW-based 1.7-liter four-cylinder engine mounted transversely, Omni featured rack-and-pinion steering, disc brakes, four-speed transaxle (with TorqueFlite optional)—all the features of the most respected imported cars. Priced at a base of $3,976, the Omni clearly showed the direction small cars were headed in.

As before, Pinto offered a Pinto station wagon. New features were split rear seats, optional variable-ration rack-and-pinion power steering and new color choices.

Popular among young singles was the Mustang II, now available with a new Fashion Accessory package in nine exterior colors. Designed especially for women, the option package included a four-way adjustable driver's seat, map pockets, illuminated entry system and a driver's side illuminated visor vanity mirror. A 2.3-liter four-cylinder engine was standard, with Ford's 2.8 V-6 or 5.0 V-8 optional.

Dodge's Aspen received new front-end styling this year, and Diplomat included a new model—a station wagon. Dodge's Cordoba clone, the Charger, looked the same this year, and was joined by another sporty two-door, the Dodge Magnum. Magnum's bold front-end styling included rectangular headlamps and a slotted grille.

As most people would guess, Plymouth also had a new subcompact this year. Its Horizon was a twin to the Dodge Omni, differing only in minor details. The Volare series was trimmed back considerably this year, consisting now only of a Volare two-door, four-door and wagon. Gone were the separate Custom and Premier designations, though enough product variation was available in the Volare line simply by surfing the option list. The full size Gran Fury was dropped, but the mid-size Fury line continued. Motor Trend named the Plymouth Horizon and Dodge Omni twins Car of the Year.

Ford at last discontinued its ancient Maverick, replacing it with the all-new Fairmont. The new compact was quite an innovative product for Ford, clearly designed to be a major volume seller. Built on an all-new chassis with a 105.5-inch wheelbase, Fairmont offered generous interior space with room for five. Careful engineering kept the curb weight around 2600 pounds, allowing Ford to power the base model with the same 2.3-liter, four-cylinder engine used in the Pinto. A better choice was the optional 200-cid in-line six-cylinder or 302 V-8. Fairmont seemed to combine the passenger space of an intermediate with the fuel economy of a subcompact. Offered in both two- and four-door sedan

1978

Top Movies

- Grease
- Superman: The Movie
- National Lampoon's Animal House
- Every Which Way But Loose
- Jaws 2

Ford's biggest news this year was the all-new Ford Fairmont, which replaced the aged Maverick. Fairmont came in two- and four-door sedans, a roomy station wagon and a sporty Futura coupe. A sporty ES trim option, shown here, was popular.

Ford offered its new Fairmont with this fuel-efficient 2.3-liter engine as standard equipment. In preliminary EPA testing, a Fairmont equipped with this engine and an automatic transmission achieved fuel-economy ratings of 33 miles per gallon on the highway, 22 mpg in the city, for a combined rating of 26 mpg.

The 100-millionth U.S.-built Ford vehicle was produced during the 1978 model run. The cream and gold 1978 Fairmont Futura was completed at Ford's Mahwah, NJ assembly plant on November 15th.

models, a sporty two-door Futura coupe, plus an attractive station wagon version, buyers could customize their cars by ordering additional equipment from Fairmont's extra long options list. Magazines raved about the Fairmont, calling it head and shoulders above the GM and Chrysler compacts. With prices that began as low as $3,589, Fairmont was bound to be a hit.

Modifications to the rest of the line were minor. Granada got a new grille this year, the LTD II station wagon was dropped, while Mustang and Pinto offered new color choices. Ford was celebrating its 75th Anniversary all year, and a Diamond Jubilee edition Thunderbird was an exciting special offering.

Lincoln's Versailles traded in its 351-cid V-8 for a 302 V-8 this year, but appearance changes were minor. The rest of the Lincoln line saw small improvements.

Mercury's Comet also bit the dust this year, and its replacement was the Mercury Zephyr, a re-

badged Ford Fairmont. Zephyr came in the same body styles as the Fairmont and offered the same drive train choices. Styling was similar, though the Zephyr came with quad rectangular headlamps, while Fairmont had only two. With its better interior trim and equipment, the Zephyr was priced a

1978
Music News

• Billy Joel releases "52nd Street," which heads to number one.

• The Styx album "The Grand Illusion" sells over three million copies.

• Canada's first major rock festival, "Canada Jam," is held in Ontario.

bit above the Fairmont, but Zephyr still represented an outstanding value. The balance of the Mercury was mostly unchanged.

Thus, for the year, GM had introduced downsized intermediates, Ford had debuted all-new, vastly more efficient compacts, and Chrysler had brought forth the first front-wheel-drive subcompacts from an American producer. These were radical changes. If the flood of new products from GM, Ford and Chrysler proved anything at all, it was that the older American cars still on the market would soon have to be redesigned to match the needs of a rapidly changing marketplace.

Things would never be the same again.

It's no wonder that Ford's newest compact sold in high numbers. Fairmont's sedan and wagon offerings were very attractive family cars, well-priced and modern.

The top of the Ford product line was still a full-size American car, the beloved LTD. Two- and four-door pillared hardtops were available in the LTD and LTD Landau series, while station wagons could be had in LTD or LTD Country Squire trim. Ford bragged that LTD was one of the few cars still capable of towing travel trailers with a loaded weight of up to 7,000 pounds. A 7.5-liter (460-cid) V-8 was optional.

Ford's LTD II continued to attract buyers interested in a traditional mid-sized American car. For 1978 LTD II offered new paint and trim colors. A 302 V-8, automatic transmission, power front disc brakes, steel-belted radial ply tires, and power steering were all standard equipment. A Citizens Band (CB) radio was a popular option.

For 1978, Lincoln Versailles got a new Dark Red Metallic color choice, plus a standard Electronic Engine Control system.

Lincoln Mark V retained its stately size and elegant appearance, and remained popular among the well-to-do.

Mercury got its own version of the new Fairmont, which it called the Zephyr. Mercury Zephyr's front-end appearance was somewhat fancier since it came with quad headlamps rather than the dual lights seen on the Ford. Zephyr offered agile handling, excellent fuel economy and clean styling. Like Fairmont, Zephyr came in a choice of four body styles.

Included in the Zephyr line-up was this sporty Z-7 two-door coupe. With its available 5.0-liter engine, the Z-7 could go 0-60 mph in about 11 seconds—excellent performance for those fuel-tight days.

One of the most hilarious TV shows of the 1970s was Taxi. Set in a grimy New York City garage, Taxi had a cast of comedy actors including Danny DeVito (left) and the late Andy Kaufman, and featured the venerable checker cab.

Oldsmobile's new Cutlass Supreme coupe was a very handsome design. Highly fuel efficient and quite comfortable, Cutlass Supreme attracted many buyers.

In 1978, the author was an Oldsmobile salesman in Milford, Connecticut and sold quite a number of these popular Cutlass Supreme coupes.

Olds' Omega was still in the line-up, offered a choice of V-6 or V-8 power.

Plymouth's big news this year was the all-new efficiency-sized Horizon. Its chiseled lines were quite appealing, and it seated four adults in comfort while delivering excellent fuel economy. A factory-installed roof rack was optional.

Horizon's functionality was enhanced by its hatchback design and available roof rack.

Small sporty coupes were a big part of the auto market, and Pontiac's Sunbird was one of the better sellers.

If buyers felt the Horizon wasn't sporty enough, Plymouth dealers still offered the Arrow, imported from Mitsubishi. The GT continued to offer a racy appearance.

Pontiac renamed its compact Phoenix this year. Although it featured styling changes, it was very similar to the previous Ventura and was still based on the Chevy Nova chassis.

The new Phoenix was offered in two-door coupe and four-door sedan models, plus a two-door hatchback. The upscale Phoenix LJ was offered only in the coupe and sedan styles. A 3.8-liter V-6 was standard on all models, but both a 2.5-liter four-cylinder engine and a 5.0-liter V-8 were available as options.

Pontiac's Gran Prix was all new this year, downsized a good bit but still an attractive sporty mid-size coupe.

Also debuting this year were Pontiac's all-new Le Mans and Grand Le Mans. As was the case with the other GM mid-size cars, the Le Mans was smaller, lighter and more fuel efficient but retained the interior roominess that Americans demanded.

Chapter Ten

1979

End of A Great Decade?

Time was running out on the'70s. Disco was still hot, but muscle cars were not. Pseudo-luxury cruisers were the machines most seen parked outside nightclubs. High heels and expensive clothes had supplanted the sandals, tie-dyed shirts and patched jeans of an earlier decade. America's culture had changed drastically in the ten-year interval.

You could see it in the movies. Winner of this year's Academy Award for Best Picture was *Kramer Vs. Kramer*, a tale about a couple's divorce fight. Copping a nomination was the depressing *Apocalypse Now*, a truly bizarre war flick about Vietnam. Almost unnoticed by many moviegoers was a really great little film, one of the best of the decade, *Breaking Away*, a story about bicycle racing and coming of age in Indiana. The great actress Sally Field put in a memorable performance as a southern textile worker in the terrific *Norma Rae*—and won an Oscar for Best Actress playing the title role. An unusual film was *Being There*, an odd little farce about a half-witted man forced to live in a world he's long been sheltered

from. Peter Sellers put in one of the best performances of his career playing the part of Chance the gardener.

The Doobie Brothers were on top of the record charts with their hit "What a Fool Believes," which won both Record of the Year and Song of the Year awards. Bob Dylan displayed his remarkable staying power with "Gotta Serve Somebody." Disco was BIG—Donna Summer had a giant hit with "Hot Stuff," while Gloria Gaynor's "I Will Survive" won the award for Best Disco Recording.

In the fall TV lineup, "60 Minutes", "Three's Company", "M*A*S*H", and "Dallas" were among the most popular.

Chevrolet didn't have much in the way of new product announcements this year. The division was preparing for the introduction of a revolutionary new front-wheel-drive compact to replace its Nova series, but the new car wouldn't be ready until the spring. At any rate, when that new car was introduced, as the Citation, it was badged as a 1980 model, and thus, for our purposes, is not considered a 70s car.

The former Sebring-Vanguard company, bankrupt Florida builder of small electric cars, was sold at auction to General Engines Co. of New Jersey. The new owners reengineered the former CitiCar and CitiVan products, and renamed them Comuta Car and Comuta Van. The 1979 Comuta Van shown here was probably made early in the model year, since later Comuta vehicles have much larger bumpers.

American Motors followed up the success of its Concord by introducing the new Spirit subcompact. Spirit was available in two body styles, a sporty liftback and this two-door Spirit Sedan, which was based on the former Gremlin.

The Spirit Liftback was by far the best selling of the two Spirit styles. Though based on the former Gremlin, Spirit Liftback had much cleaner, sportier lines. Three trim levels were offered: base, D/L and Limited (shown).

Spirit Liftback's rear opening was much larger and more convenient than the Gremlin's opening rear window.

AMX was new again this year—the third year in a row for AMC's image car. Based now on the new Spirit Liftback body, the AMX was a 2+2, not a two-seater. Bold graphics, a rear spoiler, and huge wheels and tires were main appearance features. Engines included a standard in-line six and optional 304 V-8.

For its second year on the market, AMC's Concord received new bumpers, new grille and revised vinyl roof treatments. The net effect was improved looks.

For 1979, Chevy's popular Chevette received an attractive new grille, which was more than its Monza stablemate received. However, Chevrolet engineers did manage to squeeze more horsepower out of Monza's base engine. Nova, now in its final year of production, sported a more luxurious grille and rectangular headlamps. Camaro added a new Berlinetta model, which combined luxury with sportiness. Malibu also received a new grille, plus an additional V-8 option, a 267-cid mill. Both Monte Carlo and Caprice underwent styling updates.

Buick's story for 1979 was similar, because it, too, was awaiting the introduction of a new compact. Its Skyhawk underwent new front-end styling with dual rectangular headlamps, while Skylark also got new front styling, plus a more powerful V-6 engine. Buick's Century "Aeroback" two- and four-doors sedans were selling very slowly—because the public disliked their unusual styling—so the division began to dress them up with fancier wheels and color treatments, in an effort to make them more attractive. It helped, but not much.

It was a different story with the handsome Buick Regal, though. This splendid-looking coupe was a favorite of young professionals on their way up, and easily outsold the Century. The Le Sabre, Electra and Estate Wagon all received updated styling.

Buick's big news this year was a completely new Riviera. Downsized, and now produced on a front-wheel-drive Eldorado/Toronado chassis, the new Riv could be had as a V-8 coupe, or as a hot S Type Turbo V-6 sport coupe. Either way, the new Riviera

1979

Top News Items

- The Shah is deposed, and the Ayatollah Khomeini leads an insurrection in Iran. Terrorists seize the American embassy, taking over 60 hostages.

- Sony introduces a new portable radio called a "Walkman."

- At the Three Mile Island nuclear power plant in Pennsylvania, a cooling system problem causes 100,000 people to be evacuated.

Buick was promoting its big Le Sabre coupe this year. The idea of a full-size two-door sedan has faded away over the years, and at this writing, no company produces one.

Buick's Riviera was a classy sport coupe for luxury market buyers. The big "Riv" simply oozed prestige.

was more of a sports/touring car than it had been in several years, and won acclaim from the auto press.

Cadillac Eldorado came in for downsizing this year, shrinking some 20 inches in overall length and weighing some 1100 pounds less than the prior year's model. Wheelbase was more than a foot shorter, and width was reduced by about eight inches. The new Eldo was built on a front-wheel-drive chassis and despite the downsizing, headroom and legroom were actually greater than before. Cadillac De Ville and Fleetwood received new front styling and new taillights as well as interior updates. The Seville was carried over with minor changes.

Oldsmobile was coming off a great year and looked for another one for 1979. The Oldsmobile lineup was one of the strongest and most popular in the world. Big news this year was the all-new Toronado, which shared its chassis with the new Buick Riviera and Cadillac Eldorado. Like those cars, this year's Toro was significantly smaller and lighter—by some 900 pounds—and was much more fuel efficient than before. Toronado shared the crisp, razor sharp lines of its corporate cousins, and was a very stylish luxury coupe. Like Buick, Olds dealers were having a hard time selling the "Aero-Back" styled Cutlass two- and four-door sedans—the public just didn't go for them. Olds offered special option pack-

1979
Top TV Shows

- 60 Minutes
- Three's Company
- That's Incredible
- M*A*S*H*
- Alice
- Dallas
- The Jeffersons
- The Dukes of Hazzard
- One Day at a Time

ages, which included styled wheels and discounted equipment, to spur sales.

The Olds Omega was in its last year on the market and got a revised grille to differentiate it from the previous year. Starfire got new front end styling, and the Firenza sport appearance option,

Traditional luxury sedans were still in abundance, though they were a bit smaller and more sensible than had been the case in the early '70s. The Cadillac Fleetwood Brougham D'Elegance was just right for a trip to the theater.

Berlinetta, a new luxury version of Chevrolet's sport coupe, joined the Camaro line-up in 1979.

Malibu Classic offered mid-size buyers a touch of luxury at a modest Chevy price.

Chevy Nova was similar in exterior dimensions to the more expensive Malibu, but had less interior room. New this year were rectangular headlamps. This was the final year for Nova. Its replacement, a front-wheel-drive car that would be named Citation, had already been spotted during testing by eagle-eyed journalists.

which had debuted in mid-1978, returned this year. The big Olds Eighty-Eight and Ninety-Eights returned with minor upgrades.

Oldsmobile's Cutlass Supreme was still America's most admired family car. During the 1979 model year more than 450,000 were produced. This year the division added a thrifty new 260-cid V-8 diesel as an option for its Cutlass line.

Pontiac's news was much like its corporate kin's—not much in the way of new products. Sunbird, Phoenix and LeMans received new grilles, while Firebird came in for a more in-depth re-styling of the front end. Catalina and Bonneville also benefited from a front-end re-style.

1979
Sports Highlights

- Bjorn Borg and Martina Navratilova win the men's and women's divisions at Wimbledon.

- The Pirates steal victory away from the Baltimore Orioles in the World Series, 4 games to 3.

- In Super Bowl XIV, the Pittsburgh Steelers beat the Los Angeles Rams 31-19.

American Motors Corporation, America's last independent automaker, was having a fairly good year. The Concord, introduced just the year before, was given a new grille and bumpers, and their effect was much more dramatic than one would have expected. The hot-selling Concord line was expanded to three series—base, D/L (which previously had been an option package) and Concord Limited, the plushest of the bunch. AMC's sturdy 232-cid six was standard, but a 258-cid six, a 304 V-8 and AMC's 2.0-liter, four-cylinder engine were all available.

New this year was Spirit, a subcompact replacement for the Gremlin. Spirit was offered in a two-door sedan that looked (and was) based on the former Gremlin body. More popular was the Spirit Liftback, a neat little two-door hatchback with sportier styling and nice interior appointments. Spirits were offered in the same trim levels as Concord—base, D/L and Limited. Also new was the AMX, based this year on the new Spirit Liftback body, and possessing more of the essence of the original two-seat AMX of the 1960s.

AMC's Gremlin and Matador were gone from the lineup. Pacer, which now was selling at such a low rate it was hardly worth building the car, was back with minimal changes. American Motors had forged a relationship with French auto maker

One of the best-looking big cars of the decade, the beautiful Chrysler New Yorker for 1979. Completely redesigned this year, the New Yorker was smaller than previous years, but was still a large hunk of metal. The bold grillwork and crisp lines were exceptionally handsome.

Chrysler tried to capture some of the old 300 series' magic with a new Chrysler 300, based on the Cordoba coupe.

Dodge's Omni line was expanded by the addition of the new Omni 024 coupe. A very futuristic-looking sportster, the 024 gave good performance and outstanding gas mileage.

Renault and was planning to produce a new Renault-designed car in its Wisconsin factory at some point in the future. In the meantime, AMC dealers were selling the Renault LeCar alongside the regular AMC line.

Ford had a very strong line-up for 1979. As before, Pinto and Fiesta were the entry-level small cars. Pinto was facelifted this year, with squarer fenders and a more expensive-looking grille. Fairmonts looked the same as the previous year but offered seven new exterior colors and four new vinyl top colors, plus a four-speed overdrive transmission as standard equipment to replace the former three speed box. Both Granada and LTD II received minor updates this year. But the big LTD and Country Squire were redesigned this year and, in line with industry trends, the new versions were downsized. Built now on a 114.4-inch wheelbase, the new LTD was a very handsome design. Thunderbirds featured a bolder grille.

But the really big news this year was the all-new Mustang—and what a great-looking car it was! It was built now on a larger chassis with a four-inch longer wheelbase. Gone was the styling that couldn't quite hide the old Mustang's Pinto heritage. The new Mustang seemed to have several personalities. To some, its trim, handsome lines made it resemble expensive sports-tourers from Mercedes-Benz. But purists felt it recalled the

original Mustang. The size seemed perfect. After all, in some years, Mustang had seemed too big, and in other years it had seemed too small, but everyone agreed the original Mustang was just right. And this new one seemed just right, too. Both a two-door notchback and a three-door hatchback were available. Interior roominess grew by about 20%, and yet somehow Ford engineers managed to reduce the vehicle's weight. The standard engine was a 2.3-liter four cylinder, but you could always move up to the hot, turbocharged version or the 2.8-liter V-6 or 302 V-8.

Lincoln Versailles got a reshaped roof this year, adding eight inches to its roofline for a more formal

1979

Top Movies

• Kramer vs. Kramer

• Star Trek: The Motion Picture

• The Jerk

• Rocky II

• Alien

This year, Dodge dealers had the gussied-up Aspen Sunrise coupe to offer buyers.

Up the scale in price but definitely worth every penny was the great-looking Dodge Diplomat. The Diplomat coupe was a splendid-looking machine, while the more formal Diplomat sedan offered improved comfort for passengers.

look, while Mark V added a Collectors Series with gold grille. The Continental was carried over with minor updates, though it too added a Collector series offering.

Mercury's Bobcat arrived with a new grille and rectangular headlamps. It was joined in the Mercury line by a new Capri. Unlike the well-loved Capri of earlier in the decade, this new one was an American car, based on the new Ford Mustang chassis. The appearance differences between the 'Stang and the Capri were minor—grille, trim, etc., but it brought Mercury dealers back into the small, sporty car market. Zephyrs and Monarchs returned this year with subtle changes and upgrades. The Cougar line returned with its same two- and four-door models plus the XR7 sport coupe. The Mercury Marquis received the same downsizing as its Ford LTD cousin and this year weighed about 800 pounds less than before, for improved fuel economy.

Chrysler's LeBaron saw some trim refinements this year, and a slight reshuffling of the model lineup. Cordoba carried a new grille and new paint colors, plus an exciting new "300" model that included its own unique grille. The big Chrysler Newport was a bit less big this year—downsizing had come to the big Chrysler products and the cars were smaller and weighed some 800 pounds less than before. However, the result was a really attractive-looking family sedan that seemed more in tune with the times. In addition, both the New Yorker and Fifth Avenue also got the shrink treatment. Bold "Mercedes-style" grilles and trim new exterior dimensions marked the costliest Chryslers as all-new cars, and they were very fine machines.

Dodge got a new big car this year, the St. Regis, built on a 118.5-inch wheelbase, and weighing in at about 3,600 pounds—lightweight for those days. Powered by a standard 225-cid Slant Six with 2 bbl carb., the standby 318-cid and 360-cid V-8s were optional.

Dodge also had a new small car this year, a sporty two-door hatchback, based on the Omni chassis. Called the Omni 024, it featured very futuristic and unusual styling, good handling, plus the all the benefits—i.e., front wheel drive and excellent fuel economy—seen in the regular Omni. As an image builder, the 024 was dynamite—its looks were impossible to ignore, and its combination of style, economy and performance were extremely competitive. Dodge's Omni sedan and Aspen line returned with minimal changes. The Charger was dropped, making Magnum Dodge's sole mid-size sporty model.

Plymouth also got a new small, sporty car. Called the Horizon TC3 (who thought up these names, anyway?) it was a near-twin to Dodge's Omni 024, with a slightly varied appearance. The

St. Regis was the big Dodge this year. Although not as large as Dodges of the first half of the 1970s, St. Regis was a big, plush automobile.

Ford continued to emphasize its extensive small car range. The modern and efficient Fiesta was selling decently, despite a renewed interest in larger cars.

Pinto styling was further improved this year. The Pinto Cruising Van in the background was an interesting variation.

Ford made a conscious effort to upgrade the Pinto this year and one of the results was the sporty ESS model shown here.

1979

Music News

- Supertramp issues their latest album "Breakfast in America," defining their sound in the United States.

- The Who tours with a new drummer, Kenny Jones. Their old drummer, Keith Moon, died the year before.

- Ry Cooder pioneers digital recording with his new album "Bop Till You Drop."

Volare line added an optional "Duster" package that included spoke wheels and two-tone paint plus assorted trim items. The Fury line was ushering Plymouth out of the mid-size category. Plymouth now would market only cars in the compact and subcompact sectors. Plymouth's sales volume had been cut in half since the opening of the decade.

America's other two car companies, Checker and Avanti, were both still in business and building cars, but the auto industry was getting increasingly difficult for small companies, and it was hard to imagine how these small firms would survive in the future. For now, though, both were still with us.

The editors at *Motor Trend* magazine picked the Buick Riviera S as 1979's "Car of the Year of the Year," and the handsome tourer deserved all the praise and acclaim it received—it was a beauty. Speaking of beauties, over in Atlantic City, Kylene Barker of Roanoke, Virginia was named Miss America.

On December 31, 1979, we all got together with friends and loved ones to celebrate the end of the old year and the start of a new year. We were also toasting the end of a decade, a decade of change, of tumult, and of excitement. Was it a great decade?

You know it was.

Still a favorite among American moms was the Pinto wagon, seen here with woodgrain side trim.

Ford consistently hit the right target whenever it produced a major redesign of its legendary Mustang, and 1979 is a good example. Buyers this year were looking for more than simply good gas mileage. Consumers wanted cars that were larger and more comfortable than the tiny econoboxes they had been trying to live with since 1974, and many buyers were looking for improved performance. The all-new Mustang for 1979 offered improvements in ride, handling, power, fuel economy and quality. One of the most successful Ford designs, this style stayed in production for many years.

The new Mustang offered two aerodynamically styled models this year—a two-door sedan and a three-door hatch-back. A choice of four-cylinder, V-6 or V-8 engines was available so buyers could select the one that best suited their desires. Speed control, tilt steering wheel, power door locks and a flip-up moon roof were optional. Note the 5.0 emblems on the model shown.

Ford Granada for 1979 offered revised trim and new color choices. Three Granada series were available: standard, Ghia and ESS (above).

Three of the popular Fairmont models were the two-door sedan, four-door sedan and the Futura coupe.

One car that was hard to ignore was the Ford LTD II with the Sports Appearance package shown here. Loud stripes and bold colors, plus styled wheels and large bodyside decals, made this a standout on the road.

Ford's Thunderbird represented solid value in a mid-size car, and was selling at a good clip.

The Thunderbird Heritage Edition offered top-of-the-line luxury with a long list of standard features that included a formal padded vinyl roof, monochromatic paint schemes, speed control, leather interior trim, an AM-FM radio, power windows, locks and driver's seat, and air conditioning. This would be a great car to find today.

This is what folks drove in the days before minivans. Boasting a payload capacity able to meet the demands of most suburban family needs, Ford's stylish Country Squire found many buyers. Completely redesigned for 1979, the big Ford wagon could carry standard-size 4 x 8 sheets of plywood flat on its cargo floor. Cargo capacity was an enormous 91.7 cubic feet.

At first glance, Lincoln Versailles for 1979 appeared the same as the previous year, but a new, longer roofline yielded important improvements in interior spaciousness. Other new features were integral coach lamps, larger rear doors and the first use of halogen headlamps on an American car.

The Lincoln Mark V continued to be the gold standard in the Luxury-Specialty market segment. Special models this year included a Collectors Series that commemorated the final year of the traditional full-size Mark, plus new versions of the four Designer Series Marks and nine versions of the Luxury group series.

A very popular Mark V model was this Bill Blass edition—one of the Designer Series. Named for fashion legend Bill Blass, it included special color and trim features, plus a new landau vinyl roof treatment. TV's Dallas was one of the most watched programs in the world!

Mercury Capri for 1979 was all new. Built in America now, and based on the new Ford Mustang, Capri standard equipment included a 2.3-liter four-cylinder engine, four-speed transmission, rack-and-pinion steering, and bucket seats. Capri was offered only in this three-door hatchback body style.

Sporty or posh, Capri buyers could tailor their cars to suit their fondest desires—and thousands did.

The handsome Mercury Zephyr returned with functional improvements and a broad array of new options. A new four-speed overdrive transmission became standard equipment, greatly improving Zephyr's already impressive fuel economy. New this year was optional speed control, tilt steering wheel and an electric trunk lid release.

Zephyr Z-7 was quite an attractive coupe, a good alternative for people who like sporty styling but needed room for a family.

"Sounds expensive," said this ad for a Kraco stereo. "Looks expensive" would be an apt description of the 1979 Mercury Cougar XR-7.

Oldsmobile's Starfire Firenza had debuted the previous year as a mid-year offering. It returned for 1979—and still looks good more than two decades later.

A Hurst Olds was offered this year. Although the era of the Muscle Car had passed, Oldsmobile wanted to remind buyers of its illustrious past offerings, and the Hurst Olds was welcome sight to enthusiasts.

Also recalling "the good Olds days" was this 1979 Olds 4-4-2, a performance version of Olds's Cutlass fastback two-door.

Pontiac Phoenix was in its second year, and wore styling that made it look much more expensive than it was. A new two-tone paint in four color-combinations was available.

LeMans was one of Pontiac's volume-sellers, and this Grand LeMans sedan was especially popular.

The intermediate sized sporty Grand Am front end styling recalled the great Grand Am's that appeared earlier in the 1970s.

Pontiac Firebird got quad rectangular headlamps and a restyled front-end appearance.

Horizon TC3 was unusual-looking even then, boldly modern and quite sophisticated in appearance. Its combination of economy and performance was just what buyers sought.

In retrospect, it's easy to see that the styling of Plymouth's Champ was heavily influenced by AMC's Pacer, though on a smaller platform.

Over the years, Plymouth had developed a strong lineup of small cars, including the sporty, new Horizon TC3 2+2 hatchback and the Horizon four-door hatchback, shown here with the optional sunroof.

The new Sapporo extended Plymouth's small car line further. Sapporo was a Japanese-built small coupe with a touch of luxury.

One of America's favorite pastimes was watching the great comedy series Taxi, with its band of wacky cab drivers—and mechanic Latka Gravas played by Andy Kaufman.

Auto racing wasn't as big a sport in 1979 as it is today, but it was just as exciting. Shown here are the top three finishers of the April 1, 1979 Southeastern 500. Dale Earnhardt (#2 Monte Carlo) came in first, in second place was Bobby Allison (#15 Thunderbird), and third place was taken by Darrell Waltrip (in the #88 Monte Carlo).

STANDARD CATALOG SERIES

Krause Publications' Standard Catalog series is available by specific marque, in individual volumes. Each book contains in-depth profiles of specific makes by model, factory pricing system assures readers of accurate values, whether a vehicle is a #1 low mileage, rust-free beauty or a #6 parts-only heap. "Techs & specs, " original factory prices, production and serial numbers, and engine/chassis codes are noted by model, thus helping you determine authenticity accurately.

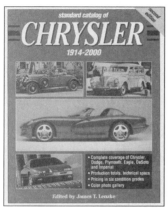

Softcover • 8-1/2 x 11 • 552 pages
500 b&w photos
8-page color section
Item# AY02 • $22.95

Softcover • 8-1/2 x 11 • 304 pages
500 b&w photos
8-page color section
Item# AK02 • $21.95

Softcover • 8-1/2 x 11 • 304 pages
600+ b&w photos
16-page color section, 36 color photos
Item# AL02 • $21.95

Softcover • 8-1/2 x 11 • 304 pages
800 b&w photos • 20 color photos
Item# SCIN1 • $21.95

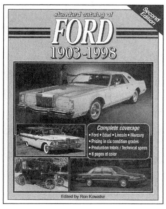

Softcover • 8-1/2 x 11 • 480 pages
1,500 b&w photos • 20 color photos
Item# AF02 • $21.95

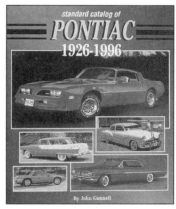

Softcover • 8-1/2 x 11 • 304 pages
800 b&w photos
Item# APO01 • $18.95

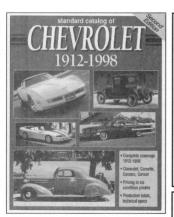

Softcover • 8-1/2 x 11
480 pages
1,000 b&w photos
Item# AV02 • $21.95

To place a credit card order or for a FREE all-product catalog
Call **800-258-0929** Offer AUBR
M-F, 7 am - 8 pm • Sat, 8 am - 2 pm, CST

Krause Publications, Offer AUBR
P.O. Box 5009, Iola, WI 54945-5009
www.krausebooks.com

Shipping and Handling: $3.25 1st book; $2 ea. add'l. Foreign orders $20.95 1st item, $5.95 each add'l.
Sales tax: CA, IA, IL, PA, TN, VA, WA, WI residents please add appropriate sales tax.
Satisfaction Guarantee: If for any reason you are not completely satisfied with your purchase, simply return it within 14 days and receive a full refund, less shipping.

Retailers call toll-free 888-457-2873 ext 880, M-F, 8 am - 5 pm

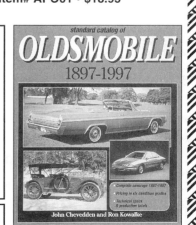

Softcover • 8-1/2 x 11
304 pages
800 b&w photos
Item# OLDS • $21.95

ULTIMATE AUTOMOTIVE REFERENCES

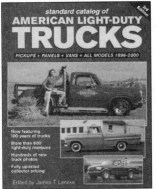

Standard Catalog™ of American Light-Duty Trucks, 1896-2000
3rd Edition
edited by James T. Lenzke
Fully research & accurately price your truck or the one you're considering with the most complete American light-truck price and identification guide. Find vehicle identification numbers, engine data, and nearly 60,000 prices based on the industry standard 1-to-6 vehicle condition rating scale. Nearly 10,000 listings & 1,300 more factory original photos.

Softcover ▪ 8-1/2 x 11 ▪ 1,008 pages
3,600+ b&w photos
Item# PT03 ▪ $34.95

2001 Standard Guide to Cars & Prices
13th Edition
edited by Ron Kowalke and Ken Buttolph
Now boasts more than 245,000 accurate, current prices in our industry-wide 1-to-6 Vehicle Condition Grading Scale for over 90 years of automobiles! From 1901 through 1993, for every model and body type of all popular American-built cars and light trucks plus imported cars, you'll find the accurate pricing info you need to buy & sell with confidence.

Softcover ▪ 6 x 9 ▪ 712 pages
200+ b&w photos
Item# CG13 ▪ $17.95

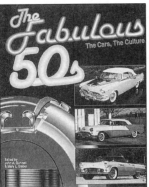

The Fabulous '50s
The Cars, The Culture
by John A. Gunnell & Mary L. Sieber
Take a walk down memory lane with John Gunnell and Mary Sieber in a photographic look at the cars that caught our fancy in the fabulous '50s. More than 500 photos, advertisements and billboards are included.

Softcover ▪ 8-1/2 x 11 ▪ 304 pages
500 b&w photos
16-page color section
Item# CF01 ▪ $14.95

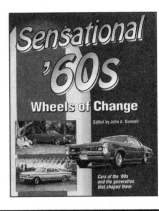

Sensational '60s
Wheels of Change
by John A. Gunnell
Cruise through the history of how the automobile helped shape America's history from 1960-1969 with more than 600 photos. Informative captions give you the facts, fads and philosophies of those turbulent years.

Softcover ▪ 8-1/2 x 11 ▪ 304 pages
600+ b&w photos
Item# SX01 ▪ $16.95

STANDARD CATALOG™ OF AMERICAN CARS

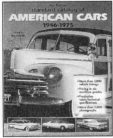

1946-1975
4th Edition
edited by Ron Kowalke
This expanded 4th edition is the source for all your questions concerning postwar collector cars. Included are technical specs, serial number information, production totals, and the all-important values of all automobiles listed in the book. From the publisher of *Old Cars Weekly News & Marketplace*.
Softcover ▪ 8-1/2 x 11 ▪ 928 pages
2,800 b&w photos ▪ 16-page color section
Item# AC04 ▪ $34.95

1805-1942
3rd Edition
edited by Beverly Rae Kimes & Henry Austin Clark, Jr.
The ultimate reference that completely details production numbers by series and body styles, giving serial numbers, engines and chassis specs. Pricing according to condition.

Softcover ▪ 8-1/2 x 11 ▪ 1,598 pages
5,000+ b&w photos
Item# AB03 ▪ $55.00

1976-1999
3rd Edition
by James M. Flammang & Ron Kowalke
Thousands of prices of vehicles in up to 6 grades of condition make this a must-have for car enthusiasts. Complete and accurate listings of production figures, options, serial numbers, technical data, specification charts, chassis information and significant historical facts.
Softcover ▪ 8-1/2 x 11 ▪ 976 pages
2,000 b&w photos ▪ 16-page color section
Item# AD03 ▪ $34.95

To place a credit card order or for a FREE all-product catalog call

800-258-0929   Offer AUBR

M-F, 7 am - 8 pm ▪ Sat, 8 am - 2 pm, CST

Krause Publications, Offer AUBR, P.O. Box 5009, Iola, WI 54945-5009
www.krausebooks.com

Shipping and Handling: $3.25 1st book; $2 ea. add'l. Foreign orders $20.95 1st item, $5.95 each add'l.
Sales tax: CA, IA, IL, PA, TN, VA, WA, WI residents please add appropriate sales tax.
Satisfaction Guarantee: If for any reason you are not completely satisfied with your purchase, simply return it within 14 days and receive a full refund, less shipping.

Retailers call toll-free 888-457-2873 ext 880, M-F, 8 am - 5 pm